The Inside Pitch
. . . and More

The Inside Pitch
. . . and More

Baseball's Business and the Public Trust

Gene A. Budig

West Virginia University Press

Morgantown 2004

West Virginia University Press, Morgantown 26506

First edition by West Virginia University Press
Printed in the United States of America

10 09 08 07 06 05 04   8 7 6 5 4 3 2

ISBN (cloth) 0-937058-85-8 (alk. paper)

Library of Congress Cataloguing-in-Publication Data
Budig, Gene A.
The Inside Pitch. ...and More / by Gene A. Budig.
p.   cm. —
1.Baseball. 2. College sports. 3. Sports. 4. Sports Social aspects. 5. Sports
Cross Cultural studies. I. Title. II. Budig, Gene A.
IN PROCESS

Library of Congress Control Number: 2003116516

Cover photo: © 2001 Brad Mangin/MLB Photos
Cover design by Alcorn Publication Design

Contents

Acknowledgments

Baseball is the ultimate team sport and, as president of the American League, I had a roster of veterans at my side. Always there to offer sage advice on the problems of the day and on essential historical perspective were former Presidents Bobby Brown and Lee MacPhail; assistants and Hall of Famers Larry Doby and Bob Gibson; long-time Senior Vice President Phyllis Merhige; Umpiring Supervisor Marty Springstead; counselor Bill Schweitzer; former baseball executive Dick Wagner; and Financial Officer Derek Irwin, who made sure the league had appreciably more than it expended.

Also there for me during "close games" were Len Coleman, former president of the National League, and his associates, Joe Black and Frank Robinson, both stars as players and human beings. Katy Feeney, the corporate memory for the senior circuit, offered reinforcement. Another one-time NL president, Bill White, freely accepted odd-hour calls for assistance.

I must acknowledge Walter J. Haas, who taught me early on about the real responsibilities of owning a Major League Baseball club. He and the members of his family were model owners of the successful Oakland Athletics.

Among the many who influenced my thoughts on the game over the years were Associated Press baseball writers Ron Blum and Ben Walker, sportswriter Mel Antonen of *USA TODAY,* sportscaster Bob Costas, columnist Bill Madden of the *New York Daily News,* sportswriter George King of the *New York Post,* television analyst and former big league pitcher Jim Kaat of YES Network, columnist Dave Anderson of the *New York Times,* columnist George Vecsey of the *New York Times,* baseball writer Murray Chass of the *New York Times*, columnist Hal Bodley of *USA TODAY*, columnist Paul White of *USA TODAY Sports Weekly*, and retired baseball writer Jerome Holtzman of the *Chicago Tribune.*

Others who frequently went out of their way to offer good-natured, but constructive criticism were Joe Morgan, the Hall of Fame second baseman for the Cincinnati Reds and analyst for ESPN, and Harold Reynolds, a former big leaguer with the Seattle Mariners and ESPN commentator.

Few did as much to support the leagues during my tenure as Tom Ostertag, general counsel for the commissioner. He knew the rules, both on the field and in the legal maze, and he never expressed an important opinion without clear reason and precise explanation, and he reviewed several technical issues for the book. It should be noted that he has been responsible for the successful defense of baseball's antitrust exemption.

Jeff White provided many of the numbers in the book; as chief financial officer for Major League Baseball, his technical assistance was invaluable. He now serves as a senior advisor to CEOs Larry Lucchino and Vince Naimoli of the Boston Red Sox and the Tampa Bay Devil Rays, respectively. David Mordkoff, a student of mine from Princeton University and now a member of the sports staff at the Associated Press in New York, provided valuable research.

Oriole executive Joe Foss and union leader Gene Orza suggested some differing, but always-helpful views on a range of relevant subjects facing the game of baseball.

Widely respected observers of the college athletic scene Bob Frederick of the University of Kansas and Gary Walters of Princeton University furnished me with fresh and detailed insights on the state of intercollegiate athletics.

Gaston Caperton, the innovative president of the College Board, encouraged me to complete this project as a scholar in residence. In return, I am giving the proceeds from the sale of the book to the National Commission on Writing in America's Schools and Colleges, an initiative of the College Board which recognizes that American education will never realize its potential as an engine of opportunity and economic growth until a writing revolution puts language and communication in their proper place in the classroom.

Gretchen Van Bloom Budig was especially helpful in recalling many events and putting them in context. She added editorial clarity to the manuscript.

Gene A. Budig

Introduction

College students are not easily fooled. More often than not, they are ready and willing to corner their professors and pose the most difficult of questions, the ones that rarely have simple answers, and the ones they would not ask of their elders outside of the classroom. It is the beauty of the collegiate experience, the exercise of inquiry that has benefited so many able and energized young minds over the years.

That being the case, I would point out that students who were enrolled in my course at Princeton University, *The Business of Sports and the Public Trust,* never exhibited any reluctance to engage in exhaustive discussions of timely and contentious issues. The reverse was true, as they studied, dissected, and debated timely subjects with some of the leading experts from the world of sports.

The students, juniors and seniors, and most with designs on careers in law and business, were at all times polite, but persistent, especially when Commissioners Allen H. "Bud" Selig, David Stern, and Gary Bettman visited for three-hour exchanges. They also engaged in open and spirited dialogue with Jerry Reinsdorf, the owner of the Chicago White Sox and the Chicago Bulls; Larry Lucchino, president of the Boston Red Sox and a Princeton graduate; and Stan

Kasten, then CEO of the Atlanta Braves, Atlanta Hawks, and Atlanta Thrashers.

Also visiting the class and entering the academic thicket with their ideas were Al Neuharth, the outspoken founder of *USA TODAY;* Brian Cashman, general manager of the New York Yankees; Paul Beeston, former president of Major League Baseball and the Toronto Blue Jays; Rod Thorn, president of the New Jersey Nets, and Emmy Award winning sports broadcaster Bob Costas.

Making the often-contentious labor case for the owners and the players were Rob Manfred, executive vice president from the Office of the Commissioner, and Gene Orza, associate counsel for the Players Association. They left no stone unturned in their presentations to the students, which preceded the 2002 baseball agreement.

It should be reported that the class was limited to 20 students a semester, giving the participants generous opportunities for substantive exchange. Active involvement was a fundamental student requirement, and many of the ideas raised, explored, and refined in the Princeton experience are incorporated in the pages that follow. The visitors limited their activity to the classroom, not giving campus-wide lectures or media interviews. It was, first and foremost, an academic experience, one in which the professor and his guests hoped to stir interest in the area of sports as a profession.

Former Dean Michael Rothschild of the Woodrow Wilson School of Public and International Affairs at Princeton University deserves to be singled out for his understanding of the need for such a course in the business of sports. An economist, he not only suggested direction and content for the course, but also took time to engage several of the guests with timely questions that only an independent-minded professor would ask.

At this juncture, I need to offer an explanation of how a former university president and professor became the seventh president of the American League in 1994, a jump that only one other person has made, Bart Giamatti, and that was in the National League. I grew up in southwest Nebraska, dreaming of replacing Jerry Coleman as the second baseman for the New York Yankees. Poor eyesight and a slow bat brought those visions to a premature end.

I went on to the University of Nebraska and earned three degrees and was hired as the governor's chief of staff. It was there, in the Nebraska statehouse, that I grew to realize that higher education offered the best opportunity for legitimate change in society and, like so many other young people in the 1960s, I thought changes were in order.

After three years in state government, I accepted an invitation to join the chancellor at NU as his assistant and as an assistant professor of educational administration and policy. It was a dream job for me. I enjoyed teaching, doing research, and working at the chancellor's side. Within six years, at age 32, I was a full professor and the chief associate in the office of academic affairs.

Then professional lightning struck. In 1972, I was asked to join Illinois State University as dean of faculties and within a year was named president. ISU was one of America's most innovative undergraduate universities and the second largest producer of elementary and secondary schoolteachers in the country. It was far ahead of the times, giving the highest priority to undergraduate teaching.

Five years later, West Virginia University approached me about the presidency at Morgantown. It was a comprehensive land-grant university with more than 23,000 students, and it had much in common with the University of Nebraska. I eventually accepted, taking a reduction in salary, but believing WVU had a unique opportunity to attack rural health and education problems.

It clearly was the right decision to move to West Virginia. There I worked with some of America's political giants, like Robert Byrd, Jennings Randolph, and Jay Rockefeller. The university did quite well in those days, attracting vast resources for coal and energy research. It recruited and enrolled large numbers of first-generation college students from the Mountain State.

In 1981, the University of Kansas asked me to return to my roots in the Midwest as chancellor. KU was regarded as one of the strongest members of the prestigious Association of American Universities in the Great Plains. It was a match that worked, culminating in thirteen years of intellectual growth for me and real progress for the institution.

During my time there, KU ranked very high in fields such as architecture, business, chemistry, city management, education, engineering, the humanities and fine arts, journalism, libraries, law, medicine, nursing, pharmacy, and social welfare; and it built one of the nation's ten largest endowments at a state university. It reached out to many promising youngsters with attractive financial aid packages, ones rich with private dollars.

Lightning struck again in 1994 when Major League Baseball "called up" a failed midget leaguer from McCook, Nebraska, to be the American League president. It was a dream come true for me, a chance to have my boyhood Yankees as one of my fourteen clubs and a chance to be a part of America's national pastime.

My sponsors were owners Ewing Kauffman of the Kansas City Royals and Gene Autry of the California Angels, two of the American League's senior and most respected voices at the time. They especially liked the idea of having an educator as league president. Earlier, the National League owners had selected Bart Giamatti, the former president of Yale University, as their CEO. (Bart and I served together on several committees of the Association of American Universities over the years, and always found time to compare notes on the state of baseball).

Mr. Kauffman and I had been friends for more than a decade, meeting once a month to discuss his favorite subjects, education and philanthropy, and my favorite hobby, baseball. He later formed one of the country's largest foundations and appointed me to the board of directors because of my years of advice on educational matters.

I was convinced that baseball was more than a game; it was a part of our national being. It pointed the way for needed change in our social institutions. During my six years as AL president, I became a friend with boyhood idols like Joe DiMaggio, Ted Williams, Mickey Mantle, and Yogi Berra, and I knew many of the modern-day players on a first-name basis. And importantly, I learned many lessons about the realities of life from them, lessons never taught in the classrooms at my universities.

1

A Matter of Time

Baseball is a game of beauty, a timeless treasure rich in lore. Or so the poets have been telling us for years. I am one of the legion who agree, and do so with a tinge of sentimentality. It is amazing how so many educated men and women have a preoccupation with the game of their parents, and how many still check the box scores in the daily newspaper and pencil in batting averages.

Roger Kahn, known for his marvelous gift of written insights on baseball, has said in *October Men* that "there is no clock" in America's pastime, as there is in football and basketball. And that, in the minds of those within Major League Baseball who crunch the numbers, is a matter of grave and growing concern.

Attendance at major league games dipped 6.1 percent in 2002, and the explanations are varied and many, depending on where you live and who you believe. Most observers agree that the economy—along with escalating ticket prices—has been a prime factor in the decline. People are spending less and conserving their resources, and they are slower to spend on nonessentials such as sports and entertainment.

The National Football League and the National Basketball Association both reported largely unchanged attendance figures during 2002–2003; the NFL reports a one percent increase while the NBA saw a decline of less than a percentage point. Both leagues, along with the National Hockey League, freely admit the competition for the entertainment dollar is fierce and there is no letup in sight, especially with the added competition coming from big-time college sports, the Internet, computer-based games, and reality television. Because Major League Baseball has so many more seats to sell, it is especially vulnerable to economic fluctuations.

Those in management who have the responsibility for paying the bills and providing a lively product are preoccupied with finding new and better ways to attract paying customers. They are especially responsive to any form of legitimate criticism. In Major League Baseball, ticket sales account for nearly 40 percent of the game's total revenue. So let us return to the matter of time, the pace of the game.

The commissioner is convinced that long games are turning off many people, especially among the ranks of the young, who favor action and plenty of it. He is rightly concerned. A brief story makes the point: A friend of mine is a New York lawyer whose firm has season tickets for the Yankees. Twice during the season he gets to use two of the tickets, and he plans an evening of bonding with his teenage son. Not this year. The son decided to stay home and play soccer with his friends, complaining, "Night baseball games last forever." My friend did use the tickets, taking an excited seventy-two-year-old father-in-law to the stadium, which underscores still another concern that the grand old game appeals disproportionately to seniors. No one can dispute the fact that baseball remains more popular with those over age fifty than it does with those under twenty.

Those who track attendance figures fear a trend, an alarming one. According to Mel Antonen of *USA TODAY,* they see a possible continuation of the slump at the gate, one that might impact other fiscal aspects of the game such as corporate sponsorships and local radio and television contracts. Companies buy expensive advertising sign packages and air time only if there are large numbers of people in the stands or beside the television or radio to see and hear them. Lower income from the gate inevitably results in a diminution of talent on the field and an unresponsive fan base.

2

Of Importance to Many

Fortunately, the game is of real importance to millions of people. More than seventy-two million men, women, and children attended Major League Baseball games in 2002, a stunning figure that surpasses the combined total of professional football, basketball, and hockey. Another thirty-five million people—a record—cleared turnstiles at minor league baseball games during the same period. Furthermore, more than 125 new minor league ballparks have been constructed since 1990, and all of them offer an intimate surrounding for families.

And there is time for needed and purposeful change. What those entrusted with the well-being of the game must do is protect its unique position of strength with the masses, while revitalizing it in appropriate ways and on a regular basis.

Baseball remains the only major professional sport that is remotely affordable to families, with an average ticket price less than half the other three premier sports. It is critical that the clubs not price fans, especially those with low and middle incomes, out of the

11

seats. Ticket prices for 2003 went up an average of nearly 4 percent to $18.81, the smallest increase since 1995. "Families represent the future of Major League Baseball," Commissioner Bud Selig told his listeners in my class at Princeton. "Nothing is more important than bringing kids to the game. Kids are our lifeblood; they are the future of the game." A family of four might spend as much as $145 attending a Major League Baseball game, including tickets, parking, peanuts, soda, and hot dogs. (More expensive frills like caps and pennants are not included.) A visit to the ballpark results in a hefty expenditure for a working family.

What Major League Baseball must do is fine-tune a more effective scheme to bring youngsters in greater numbers to the ball fields of America, especially in the inner cities. The Reviving Baseball in the Inner Cities program, a cooperative effort of Major League Baseball and of the Boys & Girls Clubs of America, shows unusual promise. The program, which teaches fundamental baseball and softball skills while promoting academic achievement and social responsibility, has grown to accommodate more than 150,000 youngsters in 167 cities over the past fourteen years. Certainly, players and owners can unite on such a fundamental matter of importance. Len Coleman and I, then presidents of the National and American Leagues, devoted endless hours to the advancement of RBI and what we learned was that no politician, business leader, or player ever refused an invitation to help us.

Owners remain convinced that the on-field product is quite attractive to many, regardless of locale, but they abhor even a tingle of complacency among their ranks. They are driven to do better, much better, even with an uncertain economy, a battered stock market, and a lingering high rate of unemployment. Most owners have met with exceptional success in the world of commerce, and they are driven people. They thrive on challenge, and have for most of their professional lives, and they are not easily intimidated. The commissioner likes to tell all that "the essence of the game is near perfect."

"The economy is a huge factor," Stan Kasten of the Atlanta Braves says. And baseball management agrees, but they also believe that tough times demand unprecedented creativity and a different type of executive at the club level. Recent years have brought the franchises a cadre of very well-educated business types. There is, without question, a new and pervasive emphasis on sophisticated analysis of all aspects of club operations, including player development and team needs. Computers are everywhere within Major League Baseball.

Some owners say a stagnant economy has done more to slow player salary growth than anything else, including the new labor agreement. They continue to believe losses are too great and payroll should be kept in line with revenues. They also note that attendance fell at twenty of the thirty venues during 2002.

3

It Is a Financial Issue

The commissioner has been tireless in his pursuit of shorter games, committing the resources of his office to bring about early, noticeable, and measurable change. It is a high priority item for him and most of the team owners who realize the financial implications of a diminished product on the diamond. Any loss of interest in baseball, especially among the younger set of fans, because of the pace of game, would be costly and hard to reinstate. One owner from a club on the West Coast believes the length of the games had cost his team at least one percentage point at the gate in 2002.

Commissioner Selig wants a regulation, nine-inning game to run an average of two hours and 45 minutes, in line with other major sporting events. He winces when talking about some of the marathons of the past. The 2003 season shows progress, with umpires moving the games along as never before. Rules, like the reaffirmation of the strike zone rule, are being enforced and stopwatches are standard. Furthermore, Selig predicts new rules in 2004, ones that will make the game friendlier to the spectators.

There are, for example, certain to be serious discussions about adopting the international rule that allows teams just one mound visit per game before they must remove a pitcher.

Perhaps the most encouraging sign that continued progress will be made is the clear indication that owners have bought in to the need for substantive reform. They see it as an economic issue, one that is hurting their revenue streams. In the past, few of them insisted that their managers pay attention to the efforts of baseball central to speed up the games. That is no longer the case. Managers have tended to operate by rote, admitting to being traditionalists and resistant to change in field operations.

4

Winners Everywhere

All streaks, whether in life or in sports, eventually come to an end. Fortunately for the owners, players, and fans there was no work stoppage in 2002, the first time since 1972 that a strike or lockout had been averted. The reasons for the new agreement were compelling.

America had changed. Its people clearly had not recovered from the deadly events of September 11, 2001, at the Twin Towers of the World Trade Center in New York and at the Pentagon in Washington. Many had felt violated and were enraged, and many had no time for anything that they perceived was not in the best interests of America.

Even the president of the United States, once the managing partner of the Texas Rangers, went out of his way to repeatedly remind the baseball establishment that any strike would be a disaster in the eyes of the general public. Its impact would be lasting. What the nation needed at the time were comfort zones, places where the citizenry could escape the lingering fear and pain of the day and feel good about something of relevance to them. They needed to be renewed with some good things, things like sports. Major League Baseball, many thought, was such a zone, a familiar friend to the workers, and especially to the people of urban America.

The tottering economy, a reason for universal unease, played a major role, too. Fans would have recoiled against the players if they would have struck, realizing the average player salary had crossed the $2.5 million mark at a time when national unemployment figures were soaring. Don Fehr, the chief of the most powerful union in professional sports, knew the vast majority of his constituents did not want to walk. They were hearing the fans who shouted from the stands and on sports talk shows they would be unforgiving if there was another work stoppage.

As with any game, the pundits had to declare winners and losers. Most thought the owners had come away with appreciably more than the players. The players did make extraordinary concessions to management, but I believe they acted in the best interests of the game, displaying an admirable commitment to the future of the sport. I further believe the players, owners, and fans all emerged as public victors. Marvin Miller, the influential retired head of the union, was troubled by the outcome; he thought the players had surrendered too much. But, Mr. Miller is the creature of a different era. Among the current leadership, both sides, to their credit, have been careful to not claim victory.

≈

5

A Quick Lesson in History

One needs to turn the clock back to early 1999 to fully understand the outcome of the labor settlement of 2002. It was, after all, a protracted process, as is often the case in a high stakes, public labor negotiation. In late 1998, the commissioner appointed a panel of independent experts, along with a dozen or so club owners, to ponder the economics of the game. The panel was asked by Commissioner Selig to recommend ways for improvement of the financial structure. The Players Association was not given membership, but its leaders were invited to meetings of the group and asked to comment on issues of discussion.

Major League Baseball was operating under a flawed economic system at the time, and many, both in and out of the game, thought its long-term continuance as a dominant American sport was at risk. There were serious financial inequities among the 30 clubs, resulting in a glaring competitive imbalance on the field of play. One did not have to have a Master of Business Administration degree from Stanford University to deduce that the teams that expended the most usually reach postseason play, and the organization that had paid the most, the New York Yankees, had won four World Series championships in a span of five years. Conversely, teams with limited resources faced drastically limited opportunities for post season play.

There was little wrong with the game itself, or so the four panel experts thought at the outset of the study. They saw a game that was drawing nearly 73 million people to MLB ballparks and, perhaps more significantly, a game that saw another 35 million men, women, and children clear turnstiles at minor league baseball venues where general interest in the game was at an imposing new high. These facts were not lost on politicians from both major political parties and leaders from all levels of government who regularly focus on the game of baseball as a matter of public business or public policy.

At the national level, that clear preoccupation with Major League Baseball was reflected in a unique and much-debated exemption from rigorous antitrust laws. The exemption was first recognized in the early 1920s when Oliver Wendell Holmes authored a Supreme Court decision on the matter. It has been challenged both judicially and legislatively by many over the years, and especially by representatives of the Players Association, but it has survived all assaults. It is certain to be assaulted again, perhaps sooner rather than later.

Governors, mayors, and state and local legislators, especially in the 1990s, usually regarded the economic health of the game and their teams as something that merited their scrutiny and involvement. They, like those before them, identified with America's favorite pastime. Politicians treat the funding of new ballparks, for example, as significant matters of public policy, and they are not reluctant to engage in high profile debate on the central issue of who pays for what. Elected officials always refer to the public good and what the people need. As one who spent many hours working with governmental leaders on the funding issues of new ballparks, I can report that these discussions all went public, they were heated and protracted, and most resulted in politically acceptable compromises.

Almost all of these debates have resulted in shared financial commitments, ones involving the clubs with their cities, counties, and states. In the final analysis, most politicians with any length of tenure in office found a way to end up on the side of baseball and in full view of media representatives at groundbreaking ceremonies (usually governors and mayors are seated next to star players, in the front row). Commissioners Stern and Bettman told my students that many of the same particulars were in play when they had facility discussions with owners, politicians, and the public at large.

Increasing numbers of influential office holders, especially in the past five years or so, have joined their constituents (the fans) to demand early and sweeping reform within Major League Baseball. They see an obvious need for greater competitive balance within MLB, and there is heightened anxiety within small-market cities. The politicians further regard these matters as legitimate public policy. In direct response to this growing unease, Commissioner Selig reached out to a small group of nationally known leaders from government, academia, and journalism and asked them for a set of unbiased suggestions, ones that could be structured for early implementation. Thus, the Commissioner's Blue Ribbon Panel on Baseball Economics was born and its impact would be significant on the eventual 2002 labor accord.

After nearly twenty months of intense deliberations and rampant speculation by the press, the panel members concluded that the current economic system of Major League Baseball had created a caste system in which only high revenue and high payroll clubs have a realistic opportunity to reach postseason. They felt strongly that the existing system was not in the best interests of the fans, the clubs, or the players.

The independent members of the Commissioner's Blue Ribbon Panel on Baseball Economics were former U. S. Senate Majority Leader George J. Mitchell, Yale President Richard C. Levin, former Chairman of the Board of Governors of the Federal Reserve System Paul Volcker, and Pulitzer Prize winning columnist George F. Will. They were tough, fair-minded, deliberative, and not easily swayed. They thrived on their diversity of views, as you might suspect. But they were of like mind in concluding in a July 2000 report:

Large and growing revenue disparities exist and are causing problems of chronic competitive imbalance.

These problems have become substantially worse during the five complete seasons since the strike-shortened 1994 season, and seem likely to remain severe unless MLB undertakes remedial actions proportional to the problem.

The limited revenue sharing and payroll tax, approved as part of the 1996 collective bargaining agreement with the Major League Baseball Players Association, did not moderate payroll disparities or improve competitive balance.

High payroll clubs completely dominate postseason play.

"The evidence to support our conclusions was sobering, but, ultimately, undeniable," Mitchell said in presenting the panel's work. "We believe that current trends cannot continue if the game is to remain an accessible, affordable, competitive national pastime, as we hope it will."

≈

6

Things Were Changing

Don Fehr is a very bright fellow who has represented the players with enormous skill over the past quarter of a century. He chooses his words and battles carefully. Leading into the 2002 rounds of discussion on a new labor agreement, he mused: "Go back and read *The Sporting News* from now to 1800-something. You'll discover there's never been enough pitching. You'll discover a significant number of teams were written off before each season started. And you'll discover that no one made any money. Somehow we have survived."

His message was unmistakable: the economic and competitive situation of the game was much the same as in years past. And, according to Rob Manfred, Executive Vice President from the Office of the Commissioner, that situation had "served the players well," thanks in no small measure to the sustained leadership of Fehr and his predecessor, Marvin Miller.

But the fundamentals were changing, without question, as the findings of the Blue Ribbon Panel of 2000 succinctly detailed. There was a growing competitive balance problem among the teams, and that was tied, in large measure, to recent and unmistakable economic shifts. Major League Baseball had severe problems, ones that were certain to impact fan interest if not addressed in a forthright manner.

Manfred told the students at the Woodrow Wilson School seminar, "profitability was, in essence, an ownership issue" and "players and fans, in most cities, are not concerned about profitability." In contrast, the clubs, the players, and the fans have a real stake in promoting competitive balance. He also said, "No player wants to play an entire career without a genuine chance to reach the World Series and, most important, fans enjoy the game most when they believe that their favorite team has a reasonable opportunity to be successful on the field."

The Blue Ribbon Panel was not the first body to consider the economics of the game. In the early 1990s, the Joint Study Committee comprised of Fehr and Selig and four independent members, two appointed by the players and two by the owners, concluded that there was no problem with competitive balance in baseball. By the end of the decade, however, the picture had changed dramatically.

Among the more startling findings of the Blue Ribbon Panel was that no team in the bottom half of payrolls had won any of the 158 playoff games played from 1995 to 1999, not a single game. Small-market teams were noncompetitors in that span of time. The panelists took note there had been industry-wide growth in revenue from 1995 to 2000, but that growth was so uneven that it had resulted in increased revenue disparity and competitive imbalance. The economic structure was outdated, permitting a growing financial gap between large- and small-market teams. One of the most outspoken critics of the economic system was David Glass who, as owner of the small-market Kansas City Royals, argued for immediate reform, for substantive changes that would begin to level the playing field. Without question, he had clout with many owners because of his history of success as CEO of Wal-Mart, the world's largest retainer.

The Blue Ribbon Panel also addressed the matter of franchise appreciation. For years, the press and the players have taken lightly the financial distress calls of the owners. It was believed that even if owners lost some money during their years of ownership, they would make it back, and then some, when they sold their clubs. That was generally the case in the 1980s and the early 1990s.

Again, things were quite different by the late 1990s. Clubs like the Yankees and the Dodgers continued to grow nicely in value, while Kansas City, Oakland, San Diego, Pittsburgh, and Florida were sold at prices insufficient to offset cumulative operating losses incurred during the period of leadership. The Yankees were valued at $600 million in 1998, while Fox paid $350 million for the Dodgers. Kansas City and Oakland sold for $95 million and $98 million, respectively. The numbers were indisputable, delivering a powerful message. Media critics fell silent on the subject of windfall profits as a result of the sale of franchises.

7

Seeds of Change Were Sown

The panel recommendations would prove to be potent seeds, ones that were quickly nurtured by newspaper columnists and radio and television commentators. The findings stirred little contentious debate; they seemed to be accepted by most opinion makers at the outset as being reasonable and deserving of action.

I believe Bob Costas might have helped pave the way for the Blue Ribbon Panel with his widely read book *Fair Ball,* published several months before the release of the panel report. His recommendations, thoughtful and comprehensive and presented during his visit to the campus, closely paralleled those of the panel members.

Among his power points, Costas said the playing field in Major League Baseball had to be leveled, and in such a way that all thirty teams have at least a fighting chance to win, necessitating a return to some financial restraint or the application of common sense business practices. He also said the teams, if they were to deserve fan loyalty, had to be something more than revolving doors for millionaires. His clarion call was unnerving to some owners and to some players: the game, if it was to survive as a viable and attractive entertainment product, had to embrace a much more comprehensive revenue sharing plan, no ifs, ands, or buts. It would not be easy and it would call for longtime warring factions, and there were a number of them, to come together and act in the best interests of the national pastime.

There was a startling difference in club broadcasting revenues in 1999, as Costas pointed out. The Yankees amassed, for example, a total of $73 million, the largest amount in MLB ($58 million from local broadcasting revenues and $15 million from the national television contract). Montreal was at the other end of the spectrum, taking in a paltry $18 million in local and national broadcasting revenues. Fans everywhere were stunned by the revenue differences.

The same was true with ticket sales revenues. Baltimore topped the list of 30 teams with revenue of nearly $73 million while the Expos, once again, were in the basement with little more than $9 million. The Orioles continued to enjoy the striking advantages of Camden Yards, the first of the new ballparks with quaint nooks and crannies and arguably the finest of the generation of retro ballyards. Such inequities made competitive balance an unreachable dream. Costas suggested giving half of each club's local money—radio, television, and ticket revenues—to its opponents, which would have narrowed considerably the gap between the haves and the have-nots. Without question, Bob Costas brought painful clarity to the enormity of the problem facing Major League Baseball through his book and numerous media interviews. The report of the Blue Ribbon Panel on Baseball Economics then delivered a detailed and compelling case for needed reform, one that struck a largely responsive chord with the fans.

≈

8

A Game on the Ropes

In support of the Blue Ribbon Report, Commissioner Selig went to Washington to offer testimony before a Congressional hearing on November 21, 2000, and asserted that "an increasing number of our clubs have become unable to successfully compete for their respective division championships, thereby making postseason appearances—let alone postseason success—an impossibility." He further said, "The enduring success of our game rests on the hope and faith of each fan that his or her team will be competitive. At the start of spring training, there no longer exists hope and faith of more than half our clubs."

Studies showed that fans from 60 to 65 percent of the Major League Baseball cities held out little hope for their teams' likely success in early 2001. These individuals, who frequent sports talk show telephone lines, were not looking forward to spring training, traditionally a time for unabashed and universal optimism. Most referred to the spreading cancer of competitive imbalance within the game. There were troubling signs that fans from the smaller markets were beginning to give up on the game, as early season ticket sales lagged in those locales.

In summary, more and more of the fans thought the competitive balance issue might be terminal without some form of early and radical treatment. They called for fundamental changes in the economic system in place within Major League Baseball. And the politicians, especially those with ambitions for higher office, were listening and sensing a change in the winds. They encouraged the owners and players to get together soon and devise strategies for needed change, insisting that matters such as greater revenue sharing, luxury taxes, salary caps, salary floors, an international draft, and growth of the game be high on the agenda.

Veteran baseball columnist Hal Bodley wrote in *USA TODAY* on November 17, 2000:

> It boils down to this: only four or five teams can afford to pay the asking price for this winter's premier free agents. And those are the teams most likely to be favored for next October's postseason. The Yankees, who just won their third consecutive World Series, had a payroll last season of more than $110 million. The Minnesota Twins were thirtieth at about sixteen million dollars, and seventeen teams had payrolls that were at least 50 percent less than the Yankees.

The train was off the track for all to see. The system was broken, unbiased analysts from the outside agreed. The shoe dropped with finality when Alex Rodriguez signed a ten-year contract with the Texas Rangers for $252 million, a figure greater by $2 million than owner Tom Hicks paid for the entire club several years later. Manny Ramirez broke the bank in Boston when he agreed to a $160 million deal with the Red Sox, and Derek Jeter followed with a $189 million signing with the New York Yankees for ten years.

The excesses of the system were turning off a growing number of fans, especially from the ranks of blue-collar workers and older people on fixed incomes. There had to be reforms in the way Major League Baseball managed its resources, or the way it allocated them, even though the game was a big business with revenues of more than $3.5 billion a year. Furthermore, economists saw an opportunity for considerable upside if corrective actions were taken. The string of stunning signings prompted Commissioner Selig to tell *Time* in December 2000 that "the inequity of this system is now so apparent" and "it has to be changed and it will be changed."

Then general manager of the Oakland A's and now an executive vice president for Major League Baseball, Sandy Alderson freely told his colleagues that small-market teams were no longer in the business of competitive baseball, but in the business of entertainment, because adroit fans knew these underfunded teams could not compete on a consistent basis. Small-market teams, he thought, had to attract fans by alternate means other than the hopes of a championship. His logic left little room for debate within the sport.

It is relevant to point out that Seattle was in the process of building a state-of-the-art retro ballpark, and the Mariners were cutting no corners. Led by John Ellis and Chuck Armstrong, management fought for a facility that would reward their fans and keep them coming in large numbers for the foreseeable future. Management made the case that the new Safeco Field would help produce enough revenue to allow the team to be competitive. Unfortunately for the Mariners, the lure of the new ballpark was not enough to keep the likes of Randy Johnson, Alex Rodriguez, or Ken Griffey, Jr. Once again, the flaws of the economic system were apparent. There was plenty of revenue within MLB, but the obvious lack of revenue sharing doomed the game's on-field competitiveness.

In fairness to Tom Hicks, a successful entrepreneur, the signing of megastar Alex Rodriguez was about more than just baseball. He was factoring in the possibilities of increasing the value of the large acreage around the ballpark at Arlington and of future naming rights for the stadium.

9

Mounting Evidence

Revenue disparities among the clubs were startling in 1999, as the Blue Ribbon Panel members documented. One of the favorite illustrations of the group was that the Montreal Expos had local revenues of $12 million compared to $176 million for the New York Yankees; and local revenues were the largest single component of a club's total income, which includes ticket sales, sponsorships, and local radio and television contracts. Another persuasive point of fact was that from 1995 to 2000, the World Series winner each year was among the five clubs with the largest payrolls. The message was clear: teams from a growing number of venues had little chance to win or even compete.

Widely quoted economist Andrew Zimbalist thought it was time to acknowledge the seriousness of competitive imbalance and do something about it. Paul Volker, a member of the independent panel, admitted to being taken back by the extent of salary escalation and the resulting competitive impact on low revenue teams.

In his book, a best seller, Costas examined the financial disparities that he believed threatened the fundamental integrity of the game. He freely offered a series of possible changes that he reasoned would protect and enhance the baseball product. Once again, many of his deep-rooted concerns coincided with those of the panelists.

Among the Blue Ribbon Panel's more substantive recommendations to MLB were these:

That clubs share at least 40 percent, and perhaps as much as 50 percent, of all local revenues under a straight pool plan.

A 50 percent competitive balance tax on club payrolls that exceed $84 million.

A "commissioner's pool" to distribute new central fund revenue to assist low-revenue clubs in meeting a minimum club payroll of $40 million.

Responses to the proposed changes of the Independent Blue Ribbon Panel on Baseball Economics within the baseball family were mixed and along party lines, meaning owners from large-market clubs were cool toward them and owners from small-market clubs saw them as necessary. The players were leery while academics and journalists were, on balance, receptive. Fans wanted the economic system fixed, but expressed little interest in the details of how to do it.

Mitchell, Levin, Volcker, and Will, in unison, called for "early and sweeping changes" in the game's economic order, insisting that competitive balance was a clear threat to the creditability of the sport. Executive Vice President Rob Manfred, MLB's chief advisor on labor matters, told the students at Princeton that the Blue Ribbon Report provided "a valuable road map" for any future changes in the economic system.

Owners from the small-market clubs argued that the immediate problems were not about total revenue, but about how the revenue was distributed. It clearly was not being distributed equally or anything close to it. They further opined that the most successful professional sports leagues were the ones that share a significant amount of revenue, or at least appreciably more than is the case in Major League Baseball. Costas and the members of the panel took special aim at broadcasting revenues, where the gap was extreme between the richest and the poorest teams. The income from national television and radio contracts was shared equally by the clubs at the time, as was income from MLB-licensed merchandise, but those receipts were not a significant portion of the game's total revenue. Many observers from the academic community were convinced that local revenue was at the heart of the economic problems dogging the game, and had to be addressed if competitive balance was to be realized.

10

Sports, a Large Enterprise

Today's sports industry is a burgeoning enterprise. It grosses billions of dollars each year, and is limited only by the creativity of the men and women who are its guardians. Commissioners Selig, Stern, and Bettman all see a "considerable upside" for the business of sports if the right people dare to take educated chances, and always put the fans first. The trio of sports leaders predicts attractive opportunities for those college graduates who are willing to work tirelessly for entry-level salaries, are highly motivated, and have majors in fields like law, business, computer science, statistics, finance, and communications. The sports leaders made aggressive pitches during their class presentations for hands-on experience as interns with professional teams and league offices.

The reach of the sports industry is international in scope, largely because of the strength and creativity of the media companies. The much-discussed relationship between sports and money is assuredly real and leaders in government are insisting on being active players. More and more, governors, legislators, and members of Congress see sports, at all levels, as a matter of increasing public interest. The commissioners from the professional sports leagues are certain to be featured whenever congressional committees pursue controversial subjects such as the use of performance-enhancing substances by players and the purported need of public resources for stadium and arena construction.

Figures vary widely on the economic impact of sports, with some estimating its range to be between $250 and $275 billion a year. Others within the circle of sports businesses believe these estimates to be too conservative. It is a matter of determining what should be counted, and not counted, and that exercise almost always results in contentious debate and infrequent resolution. Significantly, one economist of national stature ranks the sports industry as the tenth largest in the United States, ahead of industries such as chemicals, electronics, and food.

Major League Baseball alone is about to generate $4 billion a year, and Bob DuPuy, its president and CEO, sees nothing but upside if the game is thoughtful in its long-range planning. He and Selig become animated when talking about the prospects for international growth and development of the game and the sharing of Internet rights. DuPuy sees the Internet as brimming with economic possibilities. In recent years, MLB has expanded its global reach by scheduling regular season openers in Tokyo; San Juan, Puerto Rico; and Monterrey, Mexico.

Owners decided to centralize their Internet rights in January 2000 and to share all of the resulting revenue equally. At the time, some leaders within the game thought the Internet decision might prove to be as beneficial to the health of baseball as the National Football League's decision to share its national television money 40 years earlier. Time will tell whether the people at 245 Park Avenue were excessively optimistic, but I believe they made the right moves given the available data.

The Internet potential does appear to be substantial because baseball is the richest sport in terms of statistics and games. "Our ability to make the game accessible to fans will grow exponentially in the next decade," Commisioner Selig said in class. "Using technology, we can assure our fans worldwide that they will always have baseball." He contends society is in the midst of a technological revolution and "it is important that baseball stays ahead of the curve."

As an aside, it is interesting to note that spending on sports in recent times has escalated outside of the states, too. Great Britain, for example, doubled its expenditures from 1985 to 1990 to nearly $9 billion; it more than doubled them again from 1990 to 2000. Evidence shows that Canadians are spending at a rate comparable to that of Americans.

11

A Welcome Outcome

I had tickets for the game between the Cardinals and the Cubs at Wrigley Field on August 30, 2002, but gave them away to a friend, believing the game would not be played because of a player strike. Fortunately for me, and the millions of others who love baseball, the players and the owners surprised many and struck a deal, averting what would have been the continuance of a pattern of work stoppages spanning a 30-year period. Commissioner Selig and Fehr shook hands at Major League Baseball headquarters in New York, saying the new agreement would provide for greater competitive balance within the leagues. Economists thought the often-warring parties had taken a step in the right direction; it would take time to effectively measure the impact of the 2002 accord on the economic structure of baseball.

I believe the players and owners deserve special praise for the new agreement, but one cannot ignore the many unfortunate acts of the past. The generations of public discord have left the face of professional baseball scarred in the eyes of many spectators but, luckily for the game, the fans tend to be forgiving. The view that something was amiss within Major League Baseball over the years directly impacted the perception of the game and the business of the teams. It would be unfortunate if the new agreement does not provide impetus for labor and management to pull together and promote the many positive aspects of the game and to research and find creative ways to enhance the enterprise's economic future.

The new agreement should give more teams a legitimate chance to compete. It gives the low payroll clubs like Florida, Kansas City, Minnesota, Oakland, Pittsburgh, and San Diego significant revenue sharing transfers that can be used to keep their better players around longer. The new competitive balance tax should also dampen spending by the high payroll clubs. The more affluent teams will continue to still seek the cream-of-the-player crop. That will not change; it will be slowed.

The accord of 2002 does not guarantee a level playing field like the one in place at the National Football League through its farsighted sharing of national television monies and the salary cap. It does provide, however, for an enriched system of revenue sharing for a sport that a decade ago had precious little sharing of the wealth. Without question, the agreement was a needed and significant step in the right direction, according to Carl Pohlad, influential owner of the Minnesota Twins. The deal clearly penalized big spending on player salaries and gave the poorer teams a larger share of the resources. The largest impact was to be on teams in the top and bottom quarters of local revenues. The Yankees, not surprisingly, were hardest hit by the new agreement; being assessed another $30 million in revenue sharing and luxury taxes for 2003.

Specifically, the owners and the players agreed to:

Revenue sharing that will approach a billion dollars over the length of the contract. Each club will contribute 34 percent of its locally generated revenue annually to a fund that will be distributed equally to all 30 teams. Additional transfers will be made through disproportionate allocations of national broadcasting monies.

A competitive balance or luxury tax that will charge any club with a payroll of over $117 million in the first year (2003) at the rate of 17.5 percent. In the second year, the threshold will be $120.5 million, and the tax rate will be 22.5 percent for a first violation and 30 percent for a second violation. In the third year, the threshold will be $128 million, with a tax rate of 22.5 percent for a first violation, 30 percent for a second, and 40 percent for a third. In the fourth and final year, the threshold will be $136.5 million with no penalty for a first violation, 30 percent for a second, and 40 percent for a third and fourth.

No contraction or elimination of clubs for the length of the accord, and the players agreed not to oppose the contraction of two or fewer teams begining in 2007. The union did reserve the right to bargain the effects of any contraction, including how a player dispersal draft would operate, and potential compensation for the loss of jobs.

A $10 million discretionary fund for the commissioner, with each club making a $333,333 annual contribution.

A worldwide player draft, but the parties have not agreed upon the details. It was thought at the time of the agreement the draft would be operative in 2004.

A minimum salary increment of fifty percent for the players for the 2003 season, going from $200,000 to $300,000, and an enrichment of the pension plan.

A program of across-the-board, unannounced testing for steroids.

The continuance of interleague games for the length of the contract.

What most seasoned observers thought at the time of the announcement was the players had wisely agreed to a luxury tax structured to slow spending by the most affluent clubs and to a revenue sharing plan that would give millions to small-market teams. In the past, the Players Association had successfully blocked any management efforts to slow spending by the likes of the Yankees, Orioles, Red Sox, Braves, and Dodgers. But this was a new day, one that demanded unusual concessions from both the players and the owners for their own protection and the future of the sport. The fans, from Seattle to Miami, and all points between, thought, for the first time, they had been taken seriously. They felt like winners.

≈

12

Sharing the Wealth

The commissioner had a special reason to rejoice. Throughout his tenure, Commissioner Selig had argued for additional revenue sharing. He achieved a foothold in the 1966 agreement, but the 2002 deal represented real progress. Finally, some of the wealth of Major League Baseball was being passed around, to teams that soon would have a better chance to climb in the standings. The commissioner also obtained a luxury tax that might slow even the team in the Bronx. Fehr may have given more than in past negotiations, certainly more than Marvin Miller ever had, but he emerged as the undisputed leader of the most powerful union in sports. He also legitimately could lay claim to being a statesman, acting in the best interests of the game and his players. Given the realities of the situation, I believe Don Fehr did the right things for his members and the game.

Pundits thought both sides were driven to bring successful closure out of fear. A work stoppage might have resulted in at least a billion-dollar loss for the 2002 season, a financial blow the game could ill afford. The long-term damage would have been "incalculable," George W. Bush told owners at the time, and most of the players agreed. The principal points of the eventual agreement came from the recommendations of the Blue Ribbon Panel. It should be pointed out that the panelists and the owners favored a minimum team payroll, something in the $40 million range, suggesting that teams whose payrolls fell below an established level would be ineligible to receive revenue sharing payments. The players nixed the minimum payroll component, claiming it was too low and violated the spirit of a free labor market. What most of them really feared, I believe, was that a minimum threshold might lead to a maximum payroll or salary cap in some future negotiation.

In his engaging new book, *May the Best Team Win* (Brookings, 2003), Andrew Zimbalist writes, "From the perspective of improving competitive balance, there is some better news in the new labor agreement." He said, "As more revenue is transferred away from the top teams, they are likely to exhibit more cautious behavior in signing players and the bottom teams with augmented revenue are more likely to accept additional risk." He is right on the money in his assessment. One needs to remember that the club hit hardest by the 2002 labor agreement, the New York Yankees, was the only one of the 30 teams to vote against ratification. Some owners are convinced George Steinbrenner, silent but reportedly livid, eventually will challenge the accord in court, believing that his franchise has been unfairly singled out.

Labor economists regard the new agreement as a product of compromise, one that should produce some measurable change in the right direction. It certainly will not bring about the same balance or competitiveness that is seen in the National Football League. But Major League Baseball did little in the area of revenue sharing a decade ago, the principal reason for its state of crisis. Over the four-year life of the agreement, approximately one billion dollars will be moved from the richer teams to the poorer ones. Assuming reasonable management at the club level, the competitive picture has to brighten somewhat. Some restraint in salaries is also certain to come from the agreement. Professor Zimbalist correctly points out that Major League Baseball will produce in excess of $15 billion in revenue over the life of the agreement, and that will allow for redistribution of about 7 percent of the game's total resources. It is, in my view, a "constructive start" to the resolution of the competitive balance quagmire.

Despite the recent and impressive game performances of Minnesota and Oakland, the correlation between payrolls and wins and losses cannot be dismissed. That was an effective arguing point throughout the labor negotiations, and financial stress is certain to be in evidence throughout the life of the contract. The game will need further financial refinements, as the players and owners are quick to acknowledge.

I do want to single out Billy Beane and Brian Cashman, two of the new breed of general managers. Both are young and have produced sustained and unquestioned value for their owners, Steve Schott and George Steinbrenner. Both of them operate under very different circumstances.

Cashman, for example, has been careful to not squander what many realize is the clear Yankee revenue advantage. He has great resources, no one questions that, but he also has the sense to intelligently consult with the brain trust, operating primarily out of Tampa, to make sure the team does not invest in underperforming athletes. Steinbrenner has megadollars and the willingness to spend them when and where needed. It is a lethal combination, the envy of the other twenty-nine clubs. The Yankees like to grow their own talent through a well-oiled farm system, but they also are quite willing to go outside when the opportunity presents itself. Derek Jeter and Bernie Williams came to Yankee Stadium from the organizational ranks, while Roger Clemens and Mike Mussina found their way from Toronto and Baltimore.

Beane, on the other hand, has been a crafty magician, one who has invested in very good, but not in expensive talent. He prefers players—mostly young players—who fly under the radar screen and possess unbridled determination to succeed. They often do succeed in Oakland. Some stars have left for greener pastures, players like Jason Giambi, Johnny Damon, and Jason Isringhausen. A former player who relates well to the other general managers, Beane makes what many call bargain-basement deals for the Athletics, transactions that have turned into victories and championships for the Bay area. In 1999, the Athletics spent less than $6 million on player development while the Yankees invested more than $20 million. New York has spent far more on signing bonuses than Beane and the other general managers, explaining why the Yankees, in large measure, have done so well in the international market.

Both Beane and Cashman are winners, but it is the Yankee general manager who has four World Series championship rings and came within a single game of adding a fifth. Money does matter in professional sports as it does in most walks of life. The correlation between payrolls and the team standings cannot be ignored or trivialized.

≈

13

Growing the Game in the 2000s

Baseball's historic decision to integrate in 1947 came before the civil-rights movement and the actions of many businesses and industries in the United States. It also was ahead of the federal government's integration of the Armed Forces. Owners, in the past ten years, have pushed especially hard for an increase in the number of minority hires both on and off the field, and today's hiring of women and minorities compares favorably with that of major corporations. Major League Baseball feels compelled to do better, as certain of the outside critics grade the game's efforts as being no better than a B. Professional football and basketball fare much better with those who pass out grades on minority sensitivity and hiring. Owners are especially attuned to the need to add more minority managers, coaches, and general managers.

Like so many others, I am convinced that baseball is more than a game; it is a visible part of our national being. It has pointed the way for needed change in our social institutions. The entrance of Jackie Robinson with the Brooklyn Dodgers and Larry Doby with the Cleveland Indians was important in the elimination of the racial barrier in professional sports. MLB once had the wind to its back, as a sprinter ahead of the times. But it dropped the baton.

Only 22 percent of those who attend Major League Baseball games are minorities, an alarmingly low number. There should be far more African Americans and Hispanics in the seats. "Baseball should have far wider appeal to ethnic groups," Commissioner Selig has said, believing any effort to grow the game must address ways in which to enlarge the minority base of fans. It is central to any viable business plan for the sport. He also contends that MLB has taken women for granted for too long. Women, in large numbers, like baseball and deserve to be courted, treated to creative promotions at the ballpark. Many are mothers who influence how the sought after, family entertainment dollar is spent. Nearly half of those who frequent major and minor baseball parks each year are women.

Many minorities have said baseball has ignored them for years, and they have turned their interests elsewhere. They are not unreceptive to the game, but it will necessitate an organized and creative effort to reclaim them. It will take time because of other acquired tastes in sports. The Negro leagues were once very popular, and they gave blacks a chance that white baseball denied them. The games drew large and enthusiastic crowds throughout the country, and there was an energized fan base.

Major League Baseball does deserve considerable credit for its educational efforts in recent years, and most notably for an innovative program called Breaking Barriers: In Sports, in Life. Its objective is to teach school children the values and traits necessary to deal with the obstacles that will challenge their lives. The program is offered in elementary schools throughout the 30 major cities that have American and National League teams. Sharon Robinson, the daughter of the legendary Hall of Fame great, is the administrator. The youth-based initiative teaches fundamental lessons of life, while fostering an appreciation for baseball. It reaches more than 300,000 schoolchildren each year in urban America.

Many owners of MLB teams take an unfair rap. They are portrayed as being dour and greedy, and having little interest in social and educational institutions. That simply is not the case. American League owners sought me out regularly during my six years as president to talk about higher education and the many challenges it regularly faced.

They seemed to radiate when talking about the colleges and universities they, their children, and their grandchildren had attended. They cared, as reflected in their generous giving to institutions of higher education, especially in the communities where they had baseball clubs.

Owners understand the inner city and its social and economic problems and have strong opinions on what mayors, school superintendents, and college and university presidents should be doing to strengthen the fiber of urban America. They have little patience for inaction in matters that impact youngsters. Owners funnel large sums of money to minority scholarship programs and fund an increasing number of internships with their baseball clubs. They strongly encourage their players to be active in community charities and educational programs for elementary and secondary school students, and they rarely say no to legitimate requests for neighborhood assistance. Peter Angelos and George Steinbrenner are among the big contributors to their communities, supporting projects in education, health care, and the arts.

Owners, with rare exception, see higher education as a bastion of hope, and deserving of public trust and increased financial support. They often lobby on behalf of colleges and universities in their cities. They believe in the evaluation of results, whether it is in the schools or colleges or universities or at their ballparks. They preach personal accountability to many groups.

Owners are very aware of and sensitive to minority concerns and, today, they take an active hand in the hiring of more qualified women and minorities, believing it is the right thing to do and good for business. They believe minority men, women, and children are critical to the future of Major League Baseball, and several owners of big-market clubs foresee a 20 percent gain in minority attendance in the next five years. Selig says that is a realistic goal, assuming the leaders of the game come up with a thoughtful plan of action.

One needs to understand that most owners of MLB teams had accumulated considerable wealth long before entering professional sports and, to many of them, owning a baseball club was the realization of a long-held dream. In recent times, media companies have purchased baseball teams for programming purposes, and their investments usually were not emotional ones. Many owners see their investments in the game as something they can do to give back to their communities; they see their involvement as a form of public service. Some, but certainly not all, enjoy the notoriety.

≈

14

One Path to Economic Growth

Paul Beeston is a Canadian who chuckles when Americans refer to baseball as their national pastime. He believes Canada deserves at least a share of the designation. The former president of Major League Baseball and one-time chief executive officer of the Toronto Blue Jays likes to remind people that a version of baseball was being played in Canada as early as the 1830s. In truth, the United States adopted the rules of the modern game of baseball fourteen years before a pitch was thrown in Canada.

During his productive reign at MLB, Beeston pressed hard to further internationalize the game. He liked to tell his associates that globalization of baseball was underway in the 1870s when Cubans enthusiastically adopted the game. It quickly spread throughout the Caribbean and remains wildly popular today in places like Nicaragua, Mexico, the Dominican Republic, Venezuela, Puerto Rico, Panama, and Columbia.

At approximately the same time, halfway across the globe, the game was born in Japan. Amazingly, teams from the United States started to visit Japan soon after the turn of the twentieth century.

The Chicago White Sox and the New York Giants played a game there in 1913, and Casey Stengel brought a squad of all stars across the Pacific Ocean in 1922 to promote the sport. Icons like Babe Ruth, Ty Cobb, Lou Gehrig, Jimmie Fox, and Joe DiMaggio played exhibitions in Japan, too.

Major League Baseball, to be sure, has an enormous global reach. On opening day of 2003, 20 percent of the major-league players had been were born outside of the United States. In the minor leagues, half of the players were foreign-born. The game has real diversity, which adds to its worldwide appeal. In 2001, Seattle's Ichiro Suzuki of Japan became the first player in twenty-seven years to be named Most Valuable Player and Rookie of the Year in the same season. Television ratings of Major League Baseball games have soared in Japan because of Ichiro's considerable success.

And, in 2003, Hideki Matsui, Japan's highly regarded power hitter, donned the pinstripes of the New York Yankees, and an army of reporters from Japan chronicled his every move back home. TV ratings continue to rise there. The representation of foreign-born players continues to climb as more and more of them migrate from the Caribbean and Central America, and the wealth of talent in Asia continues to be tapped. Those players are among the game's finest performers like home run legend Sammy Sosa of the Chicago Cubs and Cy Young winner Pedro Martinez of the Boston Red Sox.

The commissioner likes to emphasize that baseball has been extremely well received for generations in the Caribbean and Central America, and that in 2003 the Montreal Expos played twenty-two regular-season games in San Juan. "Such a commitment will fortify the game's popularity throughout the region," Selig has declared. "Equally important is our efforts to take the game overseas." The regular season has been opened with games in Monterrey, Mexico; Tokyo; and San Juan, Puerto Rico in recent years.

One of the more remarkable international experiences came in 1999, when the Baltimore Orioles visited Havana to play the talented Cuban National Team. Organized by MLB and with the support of the U. S. Department of State, the Orioles won a hard fought game as the event, witnessed by Fidel Castro, drew considerable worldwide attention for baseball. At a dinner hosted by the Cuban president at his official residence the night before, Castro exchanged hours of baseball stories with Bud Selig, Peter Angelos, Len Coleman, and me. There was no reference to politics, by either side.

"The globalization of the game has become one of Major League Baseball's highest priorities," Beeston said before resigning his position in 2002. "It is one of the ways we will grow the game in terms of popularity and revenue." The sport's worldwide popularity has increased steadily over the years, first through members of the American Armed Forces who introduced the game in Europe and in other parts of the globe during World War II and later through the introduction of organizations like Little League Baseball.

There are ten professional baseball leagues outside the Continental United States and Canada. They are in Japan, Taiwan, Korea, Australia, Mexico, the Dominican Republic, Puerto Rico, Venezuela, Nicaragua, and Italy. All are flourishing. Through the aggressive efforts of Major League Baseball International, a subsidiary of MLB, the game has a global television following.

The game's signature events, the World Series and the All-Star Game, are televised to more than 200 countries around the world, which is triple the number of countries that received the games nine years ago. Major League Baseball International allows regular season games to be broadcast throughout Europe, the United Kingdom, Asia, and Latin America. It now sells the rights worldwide, and revenues from those rights have more than tripled in the past decade. It is another piece of the overall strategy to grow the value of the on-field product.

The 2000 Centennial Year was Major League Baseball's most ambitious year in terms of international scheduling. In addition to the opener in Japan, MLB celebrated its Latin roots during spring training with a series of exhibition games played in the Dominican Republic, Venezuela, and Mexico. The games in Japan were instant sellouts.

To enhance global interest and participation, MLB International operates the Envoy Program, an initiative that brings high school and college baseball coaches to various parts of the world to teach youngsters how to play the game. In 2000, the program made its first trip to China, a country with a budding interest in the sport. MLB International also sponsors Pitch, Hit and Run, a program that teaches the fundamentals of baseball to elementary school children. It reached more than 500,000 boys and girls in six countries in 2000 alone.

Major League Baseball also plays the lead role in the selection and operation of the United States baseball team at the Olympics. At the Sydney, Australia, Games in 2000, a scrappy team primarily made up of minor leaguers and amateur players won the gold medal for Manager Tommy Lasorda, a Hall of Famer who inspired his players and a grateful nation.

Beeston, who detailed his strategies with Larry Lucchino in the Princeton class, forged strong ties with Don Fehr and the Players Association around the importance of international play. They agreed that global attention would result in an enlarged fan base, more youngsters playing the game, and greater overall revenues in the long run.

Fehr is an active member of the board of directors of the United States Olympic Committee, and he favors a World Cup for baseball, similar to the one that exists for soccer. He argues passionately there are enough outstanding baseball players around the world to ensure stiff competition and enough interest to ensure a worldwide television audience. Len Coleman and I always thought he was right on this issue and said so publicly.

One of Paul Beeston's goals was the fervent hope that Major League Baseball would someday be known as the international pastime. With that enlarged designation, he reasoned, would come new and needed streams of revenue for the game, assuring its future for the generations. He further believes the game has universal appeal when properly introduced and taught to the very young. Surveys always cite baseball as one of the sports with the greatest global potential.

15

A Game Set Apart

Major League Baseball has been part of American life for a very long time, since the Cincinnati Red Stockings began playing in 1869. Its long history sets the game apart from other professional team sports of the day, and it is, as we will explore, a mixed blessing. We live in a competitive world, to be sure, one that demands frequent change. This is especially true in the world of sports where baseball must do battle for the entertainment dollar with the other professional and college games, television, movies, theater, music, video games, and the Internet.

Unlike the other sports, Major League Baseball must compete with its past. Fans and the working press judge the game's business and operational decisions with an eye on its history, on how things once were. The fans and the media can be harsh, even brutal on occasion, in judging the game and the people who dare to instigate changes in it. "For as long as the game exists, it will be regarded differently from other sports because of its place in the hearts and memories of the American public," Richard Levin, the senior vice president who explains many of MLB's actions to a sometimes skeptical public, said at Princeton.

Baseball, for example, is more popular than at any time in its long history. The attendance numbers do not lie. And yet much of the conversation about the game tends to center on its problems, such as the pace of the game, the on-field conduct of players, revenue sharing, and competitive balance. Not many of those who are doing the talking on sports radio and television are reveling in the sport's great renaissance, as reflected in high attendance at both major and minor league games. Their moving targets are billionaire owners and millionaire players.

Furthermore, there is heightened and well-documented interest in the game outside of the United States and Canada, and there are a record number of club programs designed to reach out to families and youngsters. The message from the general public has been heard and incorporated in programming. Significantly, there is a long line of individuals who have expressed an interest in buying minor league baseball clubs, regarding them as attractive investments for the long run. These numbers do not lie either.

It is true, without question, that the enduring success of Major League Baseball rests on the hope of each fan that his or her team has a chance to win, an opportunity to reach postseason play. Don Fehr and Commissioner Selig certainly agree on this. Imbalance among the teams does pose a chilling threat to the game, and that fact drives the commissioner's agenda of things that must be fixed, and soon. The fans have a legitimate right to be concerned and to agitate for reform, and the media has reason to be critical; that is understandable.

The rebirth of Major League Baseball began in September 1995 as fans became transfixed on Cal Ripken's determined drive to break Lou Gehrig's consecutive games played streak. The fans and the media were mesmerized by the chase, resulting in an unprecedented outpouring of goodwill. It clearly helped to wash away many of the unfortunate memories of a crippling player strike that had wiped out the last six weeks of the 1994 season and resulted in the cancellation of the World Series for the first time since 1904.

A former college basketball player at UCLA and sportswriter in Los Angeles, Levin says the Ripken achievement "did much to revive America's interest in baseball." He also gives generous credit to the introduction of the 1995 Division Series, a new round of playoffs that featured the three division winners and a wild card team competing for the chance to advance to the League Championship Series. "Initially, the decision to restructure the leagues and add a tier of playoffs was met with substantial criticism from so-called traditionalists among the fans and the media," Levin remembers.

As president of the American League at the time, I thought the restructuring, though controversial, made business and operational sense. I also thought the fans would eventually embrace it once they saw it in operation, and I was correct. The time was right for change, and later poll numbers were overwhelming in favor of the alteration. Importantly, the move improved geographical alignments, removed many problems with scheduling and team travel, and doubled, from four to eight, the number of teams that advanced to postseason. Those in marketing said from the outset it was the right strategy, one that would win over many more fans. Some of the owners were less certain, but willing to give it a chance.

Another significant change in the game came in 1997 with the introduction of interleague play, a dramatic departure from Major League Baseball's time-honored traditions. Critics, and there were many, were spewing their venom on all of the sports talk shows. "Fans and media alike initially thought that regular season interleague play would cheapen the significance of the World Series," Levin recalls. "That has not been the case." Fans liked the experiment, buying record numbers of tickets, and more and more journalists grew to accept it. Interleague play brought out boisterous league loyalists who welcomed the opportunity to wager against the other side. Average attendance at interleague games has easily exceeded average attendance at intraleague games.

However, after seven years, I do believe the commissioner would be wise to revisit the interleague matter on a regular basis, determining whether too many of the games are being played and how they are impacting the outcome of the regular season. More and more managers and players seem to regard the interleague games as a distraction.

Levin who, as part of his job, measures public opinion, believes the two greatest moments in the comeback of the game after 1994 were the homerun duel between Mark McGwire and Sammy Sosa in 1998 and the announcement of the All-Century Team in 1999. Most baseball beat reporters would agree with that assessment since both events honored the storied past while looking forward to a future with promise. The homerun chase focused on the single season record of Roger Maris who had bested the mark of Babe Ruth in 1961. I believe the homerun derby of 1998 brought deserved and universal attention to Sosa's Hispanic heritage and the value of foreign-born players.

There were few dry eyes among the 34,000 fans that crowded Fenway Park when Ted Williams and the other members of the All-Century Team were introduced at the All-Star Game. It was a moment to remember, a time when the modern-day star players met, face- to-face, with their game's history. The legends looked ageless, I thought. There was Hank Aaron, Willie Mays, Harmon Killebrew, Frank and Brooks Robinson, Stan Musial, Ernie Banks, Bob Feller, Warren Spahn, Bob Gibson, Robin Roberts, Carl Yastrzemski, Reggie Jackson, and so many more.

As an aside, the All-Star Game of 1999 generated more than $75 million for the ailing Boston economy, and the 2003 Classic bettered the Chicago economy by approximately $ 85 million.

Adding perspective through the use of numbers, Levin likes to turn the clock back to 1949 when the people of New York thought baseball was at its zenith The city had three teams, the Yankees, Dodgers, and Giants, and they drew a combined attendance of 5,113,869 that year. In 2000, the Yankees and the Mets attracted 6,027,878 paying spectators during the regular season. When Walter O'Malley moved the Dodgers from Brooklyn to Los Angeles, they amazed the baseball world by regularly drawing more than 2 million fans a season. Today, clubs average 2.5 million fans a season. Levin's message to the owners is to do everything possible to keep the game affordable, especially for the kids and their moms and dads, and to accelerate organized efforts in encouraging youngsters everywhere to play baseball as a means of cultivating future players and fans.

Above everything else, baseball is a family game, one that has been passed down from generation to generation. A clear majority of today's fans, poll after poll reminds us, can trace their interest in the sport back to an older family member. Who can forget the sights and smells of their first visit to a ballpark?

Interest in college baseball has grown dramatically in the past fifteen years, with the major athletic conferences all reporting significant and enthusiastic crowds. The College World Series, which has been held in Omaha, Nebraska, since 1950, has become one of the National Collegiate Athletic Association's most popular championship events, drawing sell-out crowds of more than 24,000 people a game for a week and millions more from national television. A number of the participants, like Barry Bonds and Roger Clemens, have gone on to wear uniforms of Major League Baseball teams.

≈

16

Where It All Started

Larry Lucchino deserves to be remembered as the person who set off the retro revolution in ballpark architecture, a movement that began in the late 1980s and has resulted in the construction of more than $5 billion worth of new facilities for America's pastime. Then president and chief executive officer of the Baltimore Orioles, he wanted a new facility at Camden Yards that would be for baseball use only, one that would have personality, charm, and distinctiveness, not the generic multipurpose stadium that had been the standard in the 1960s and 1970s.

Lucchino was determined to not share a facility with professional football. "I had noted that the one common thread of consistently successful franchises was that they played in baseball-only ballparks," he told the students at Princeton.

He had the clear vision of a new ballpark that would be traditional, old-fashioned, and an important part of the revitalization of downtown Baltimore. Quite frankly, he saw it as the likely crown jewel of the Inner Harbor. Lucchino envisioned a ballpark sited near shops, eateries, and cultural attractions, and a location that would encourage new residential and commercial development. His dream was exceeded by a wide margin.

The idea of Camden Yards caught the early and favorable attention of business and industrial leaders who liked the fact that the proposed site was near the main highways and the trains and the light rail. Everything seemed to fit. Even the preservationists found reason to be supportive. As Lucchino has said, "The political stars were aligned perfectly in Baltimore." The city had a strong mayor, William Schaefer, who would become an even stronger governor, and he liked the ballpark scheme and the long-term potential it offered. Clearly, he was the political driving force for Camden Yards, which was essentially one hundred percent publicly funded. The editorial pages of the major regional newspapers all said Schaefer had galvanized the political will for the eventual showpiece. The late Edward Bennett Williams, then owner of the Orioles, played an early and needed role in the process.

The club was the tenant, the Maryland Stadium Authority was the landlord, and Lucchino concentrated his efforts on negotiating a favorable lease and providing the needed resources for a competitive team. Politicians from both major political parties universally pointed to Oriole Park as one of the city's finest architectural achievements and tourist attractions, spurring widespread neighborhood revitalization. Commissioner Selig has said for years that Camden Yards led the communities with Major League Baseball teams to think of ballparks as more than just bowls where athletic games were held.

Baltimore's new ballpark, which opened in 1992, was artfully designed to look like an old urban park, a red brick structure in a warehouse neighborhood. Its playing field was asymmetrical, much like the ones of the past. This was what baseball parks were meant to be, journalists from across the country would write. *Boston Globe* columnist Bob Ryan likened Camden Yards to Fenway Park, the ultimate compliment. It proved, beyond question, that the best of the old and the new could be brought together in a way to please the people who bought the tickets.

Camden Yards showed the inner cities of the United States that a ballpark situated in a thriving urban neighborhood could lead to a safer community, a matter of real concern to some critics at the time of its construction. Busy streets, ones filled with happy and responsible people, are not likely targets for crime, especially if they are well-patrolled by police. Ballparks surrounded by restaurants and shops are likely to be safe havens for youngsters and their parents. Baltimore law enforcement officers have reported relatively little crime in the area of Oriole Park, which is well-lighted.

There is no doubt that Camden Yards and Jacobs Field in Cleveland have been prime drivers in the revitalization of the downtown areas and the image of their cities. Dick Jacobs, the former owner of the Indians and a highly successful land developer, liked to say that Cleveland's downtown renaissance was spirited by more than a new stadium; it had two, one for the Indians and one for the Cavaliers of the National Basketball Association. It has since added a third, a stadium for the Browns of the National Football League.

During my presidency of the American League (1994–2000), the staff followed a simple, but highly effective, procedure when communities called and wanted to explore the possibilities of a new ballpark. We arranged for their governor, mayor, and community leaders, along with their club's owner, to visit either Baltimore or Cleveland and see firsthand what a new state-of-the-art facility could mean for the community. With rare exception, the delegations would leave after thorough discussions and tours with a newfound energy and a willingness to embark upon the long and difficult process of persuading a questioning citizenry of the merits of a new ballpark.

I found Peter Angelos to be especially effective in detailing the benefits of Oriole Park, and he left no question unanswered. He was an ideal host, picking up the tabs for countless meals and beverages for the visiting luminaries. He contributed, as few others have, to the realization of many new and improved sports facilities over the years.

In 1994, Lucchino moved on to San Diego, where he joined John Moores and the Padres for a long, and sometimes painful, drive for a new ballpark. This was not Baltimore and it was not the late 1980s. It would take all that he had learned in Maryland, and then some, but he would prevail. San Diego will occupy a new $362 million baseball-only ballpark in 2004.

The Padres were careful not to build their case for a new ballpark on economic promises alone, though they did talk at considerable length about the likely overall benefits to business, as measured by jobs, income, and investment in the area. Moores and Lucchino masterfully played upon the theme of what a new ballpark could do for the area's quality of life.

One needs to understand that professional sports leagues are a business, but they are also a unique form of commerce. True, they sell entertainment in slick packages, but they also sell community identity and involvement. Richard Berkeley, a former mayor of Kansas City and a friend from my days at the University of Kansas, supported the construction of a new ballpark for the Royals and a new football stadium for the Chiefs. He liked to say, "We share the glory of their victories. We share the bitterness of their defeats. It is because we, the citizens of Kansas City, share so much with our teams that we are willing to make public investments in stadia." He wisely never attempted to sell the need for a new ballpark or stadium on purely economic benefits. That was only a part of his equation.

Too many proponents of new baseball parks have rested their cases on economic grounds, which has proven to be a questionable strategy. Major League Baseball teams are not among the big employers in the urban centers. Surprisingly, a club, on average, employs fewer than 200 people in the front office on a year-round basis and counts annual revenues of less than $135 million. This does not mean, however, that the teams do not have enormous impact on their communities, because they do. Major League Baseball teams can be very important sources of community attention and pride and focal points of the national media. Employers will tell you the presence of professional sports teams is a valuable asset in the recruitment and retention of outstanding associates. As one insurance executive from Atlanta explained, "It helps to be regarded as big time in so many intangible ways."

Scholars are divided on the issue of whether public funds should be used to build new ballparks. Some have contended that it is appropriate, and investments in sports facilities are prudent public policy. Others have been adamantly opposed. One thing is certain: the expenditures for new ballparks represent a lot of money, both public and private. Major League Baseball clubs have built seventeen baseball-only stadiums since 1989, at an average cost of about $300 million.

Not surprisingly, when stadium projects are voted upon the campaign is usually heated and the outcome is often close. Mandates in today's uneasy economic climate are something of the past, and a handful of votes can make the difference, which underscores the importance of an open and honest campaign, one based on facts and accurate financial data.

The San Diego campaign for a new ballpark brought out some interesting people and some surprising ideas. George Will is a conservative who has a legion of disciples from across the country; and many of them, true believers, quote his columns in newspapers and magazines and his commentaries on national television as the final word. Then how, you might ask, could this oracle of conservatism have favored the use of public funds to help construct a baseball park in San Diego? With no hesitation, he explained:

"Government has no business going into business. Government does have, and for two centuries in this country has had, a vital role in providing the infrastructure that makes business possible. No one in the world objects to the fact the City of San Diego builds an airport so that private entities—American, United, Delta, and Southwest Airlines—can serve San Diego. The same is true with the ballpark. All that is being provided is the basic physical infrastructure that will become productive through a private business, generating tax revenues to make the community flourish."

Will knows the game of baseball and has special reverence for its history, serving on the board of directors of both the Orioles and the Padres. He also was a member of the Independent Blue Ribbon Panel on Baseball Economics. It can be said that he understands the complex economic issues facing Major League Baseball as not many others in his profession do.

Over the years, a growing number of owners from professional clubs have threatened to pull up stakes and relocate unless there were major commitments for public financing for new or renovated facilities, claiming it was the only way they could remain competitive. Such threats, without exception, always unnerve the public and result in at least some initial outpouring of support for new facilities. Since 1980, only a handful of communities have actually lost teams and none of them have been Major League Baseball clubs. It is true there is a well-documented surplus of urban centers that are seeking teams from the four major professional sports leagues.

Larry Lucchino, by the way, now has offices at Fenway Park, where he joined the new Red Sox ownership team of John Henry and Tom Werner in 2002. As president and chief executive officer of the historic Boston franchise, he ironically must determine what should be done with one of the game's two oldest ballparks. It will not be an easy call, as many fans and journalists regard Fenway and Wrigley Field as untouchable pillars of the sport. One sportswriter has even referred to Fenway Park as the "summer cathedral at 4 Yawkey Way."

17

Twice a Winner

John McHale, Jr. has ridden the bronco twice, once in Denver and once in Detroit, and both times he has more than survived the ups and downs of fierce competition. He has recorded hard fought, rodeolike victories, finding himself in the winner's circle with new Major League Baseball ballparks. He has achieved what few others have even attempted, let alone done.

A former executive with the Colorado Rockies and the Detroit Tigers and football letter winner at Notre Dame, McHale turns almost clinical when discussing the dos and don'ts of how to pursue the building of a major sports facility, especially given the harsh realities of the day. He knows the history of public investment in such community structures.

The story begins in 1928 when the voters of Cleveland approved an urban renewal project for a downtown lakefront stadium, hoping to bring the 1932 Olympics to their state. The international games went to Los Angeles, but the project for a massive stadium continued as planned. Municipal Stadium, with seating for 78,000 fans, was completed in 1931.

The Cleveland Indians played their first game in Municipal Stadium on July 31, 1932, and, importantly, became the first Major League Baseball team to play in a publicly funded ballpark. It was municipally owned.

Even when the Indians became full-time tenants in 1946, they were the only one of the sixteen Major League Baseball teams to play in a facility built with public monies. The Cleveland voters, long recognized for their love of professional sports, had made history, setting the stage for what was to follow in terms of public financing for sporting facilities. Another significant development came in 1949 when the citizens of Milwaukee voted to approve bonds for a new stadium, hoping to attract a Major League Baseball club from another city. They were successful, bringing the old Boston Braves, then a weak member of the National League, to the state of Wisconsin. On March 18, 1953, the Boston Braves became the first MLB club to relocate since Baltimore in 1903, moving to New York. That team, known as the Highlanders, eventually became the New York Yankees.

McHale points out that when the Milwaukee Braves opened County Stadium on April 6, 1953, they were only the second team to occupy a public-financed stadium. Others would follow the pioneering leads of Cleveland and Milwaukee. He further explained:

"Things were changing in Major League Baseball. One needs to revisit the arrangements that brought the Dodgers and the Giants to California in 1958. The game was expanding from sixteen to twenty teams in 1960, and the terms of the expansion were significant. There was a growing view by the clubs, cities, counties, and states that their financial and developmental interests might be best served with new stadium projects. This was the time when millions of people began to believe that quality of life and the economics of sports were matters in tandem."

By 1996, the clear majority of Major League Baseball teams played in structures financed, at least in part, with public funds, and a number of them were configured for use by several sports. Public financing has come largely through the ability of local and state governments to issue tax-exempt bonds.

A community cannot afford to cut corners when building a modern-day sports facility, as Commissioners Selig, Stern, and Bettman each said at Princeton University. The investment is too great. These unique and high-tech structures must be built to pass the test of time, and they are, without question, symbols of pride for the citizens. A new baseball or football stadium for a big-time team costs, on average, in the neighborhood of $350 million, while a new basketball and hockey arena will run around $250 million.

During the 1990s, nearly $7 billion of public monies was expended for the construction of professional sports facilities, and all of the sports building projects were controversial, some more than others. Another $4.7 billion of public funds has been approved for additional ballparks, arenas, and stadiums to be completed by 2005.

McHale came to realize early in his baseball career as an administrator that the likelihood of reaching postseason play, let alone the World Series, was remote without competitive salaries for players, and that revenue for expensive on-field personnel had to come from monies generated at the club or local level. New ballparks came to be an enticing source for much-needed new revenues for the clubs.

Driven by the stark economic realities of Major League Baseball, he committed himself to campaigns for new sports venues in Denver and, later, in Detroit. In the Motor City, McHale, then president and CEO of the struggling Tigers, had the immediate responsibility to chart and execute a blueprint for action. He consulted with owner Michael Ilitch, once a promising baseball prospect in the minor leagues, on numerous occasions, but he understood who was expected to deliver a new ballpark, one that would give the fabled franchise new life. As American League president, I worked closely with him on the project, especially in the phase where technical explanations were given to local and state officials, and I never ceased to be amazed by his grace under fire. He refused to show even a hint of anger over what I saw as egregious behavior by more than a few individuals from the community.

McHale freely told community leaders, as well as members of the sports press corps, that a new ballpark would provide needed short-term relief for the Tigers, but that Major League Baseball had to address the long-term issues of enhanced revenue sharing and growing competitive imbalance. Most bought into his analysis and conclusions. He would say the debate over a new home for the Tigers revolved around far more than just an economic issue, believing the city of Detroit had to determine how it wanted to be viewed by the state and the nation in the long run. It was not a simple issue for many of the taxpayers, with a considerable amount of discussion, especially at the end of the drive, centering on quality of life considerations.

To the resounding credit of both McHale and Ilitch, they actively encouraged public participation in the process, knowing that any deal would necessitate a favorable public vote. I sensed considerable tension within the community during my regular visits, but it was, without question, a necessary part of the process. The people had to understand and accept any decision on public funding for a replacement to the ancient Tiger Stadium.

In the final analysis, the city, the state, and the Tigers all gave up ground and structured an acceptable compromise for a new Comerica Park. There was no substitute for public investment in Detroit. The people and the media understood and most were satisfied. Perhaps the most persuasive argument for the new ballpark was the one set forth years earlier in Baltimore and Cleveland; a new ballpark likely will trigger economic redevelopment of once-decaying business districts and neighborhoods.

Leaders from the minority community of Detroit were especially generous with their support of that proposition, and for good reason. They knew a significant construction project, like the one being proposed, would mean jobs for a community then ravaged by unemployment, and it would result in increased opportunities for minority contractors, for small minority-and women-owned companies. Always vigilant political leaders sensed the growing sentiment and acted accordingly.

Ilitch, throughout the campaign, kept reminding the community that any new baseball structure would be located downtown, and situated in a way as to encourage other business development. He saw the park bringing back long lines of fans from the suburbs, people who would spend freely at downtown shops and restaurants. McHale was joined by many of the area's minority ministers who even spoke in favor of the new ballpark from their pulpits on Sundays. "Their influence made a real difference," McHale would later declare.

Drayton McLane, owner of the Astros, tells a similar story when he recounts the drive for a new ballpark in Houston. He gives considerable credit to the minority community, and especially to the minority ministers who never wavered in their enthusiasm. Len Coleman, then president of the National League and an African American, worked effectively with leaders of the minority community on the project, which McLane says was essential to the club's financial success. Most of the new stadiums, it deserves mentioning, serve as modern minimalls, offering gift and memorabilia shops and a variety of food outlets.

Old Tiger Stadium had a scarcity of luxury seating and other amenities, and those glaring deficiencies resulted in inadequate income for the Tigers; and McHale reminded his audiences that without significant upgrades in facilities Detroit would continue to be at a severe disadvantage. The same argument was used effectively in the other drives for new ballparks, with a clear reminder from management that enhanced revenues from the high rollers would mean lower general admission ticket prices for kids.

The Detroit Lions of the National Football League have since followed the Tigers downtown, building a new state-of-the-art stadium next door to Comerica Park. The clubs share parking and security. Obviously, the Ilitch strategy for inner-city revitalization in Detroit has taken hold.

McHale firmly believes the Tigers did far more than build a ballpark; they cemented a lasting relationship with business, industry, and the minority community. These men and women have become advocates for the American League entry into Detroit and they, and the many people they influence, buy tickets to baseball games. The fan base has been enlarged through the individuals who were associated with the project. The Tigers built needed bridges to the people of color, putting in place new hiring policies that are sensitive to minorities.

As an interesting aside, owner Jerry McMorris of the Colorado Rockies, who worked closely with McHale on the Denver ballpark, asserts that if the building of Coors Field were put to a vote today, it would draw a favorable response from 90 percent of the electorate. The people have seen what a positive impact the field has had on downtown. Fifty-three percent originally voted in the affirmative, and that was without the benefit of hindsight.

Not surprisingly, some of the critics have not given up in Detroit, especially with the win-loss records of the team since the opening of Comerica Park. They regularly remind sports talk radio show listeners that the Tigers play in a facility completed in 2000, one where only 1.5 million fans bought tickets to attend in 2002, and a structure erected with the assistance of more than $160 million of public monies (the total cost was $330 million). They obviously would favor another vote (the public voted favorably twice), which will not happen. What the Tigers need most is a return to competitiveness under the direction of a popular manager, Alan Trammell. Detroit remains a "very good baseball town."

A footnote: John McHale, Jr. left the Tigers in 2001 and joined the Tampa Bay Devil Rays as chief operating officer. Today, he is an executive vice president for administration at Major League Baseball in New York.

18

The People Who Run the Game

There is no shortage of published materials on owners of Major League Baseball clubs, and what many studies have concluded is no two are that much alike. Most of the owners seem to resent any systematic attempt to compare themselves with their peers. They infrequently return student questionnaires. I do believe that any serious fan of the game should have at least a feel for the individuals who control the entity that means so much to so many men, women, and children.

One of the more interesting owners, I believe, is Jerry Reinsdorf who controls both the White Sox and the Bulls in Chicago. He has been in Major League Baseball for more than twenty years and has witnessed enormous change, living through forty-two changes in club ownership, seven league presidents, and five commissioners.

During his visit to my class, Reinsdorf said that stable leadership, on the other hand, had advantaged the Players Association over the years. He pointed to the lengthy tours of duty for Marvin Miller, Don Fehr, and Gene Orza. "This has made the owners easy prey in the past," he observed. Informed sportswriters, who have reported on the labor negotiations over the years, agree, believing the tenure issue has impacted the direction of the sport in significant ways, but most dramatically in terms of player salaries. It should be pointed out that baseball management has substituted freely on its team of negotiators in past labor agreement discussions, having a somewhat limited corporate memory.

Reinsdorf anticipates no letup in turnover among the ranks of the club owners. "There might even be more when the new owners realize what they have bought into," he said. He sees significantly more corporate ownership on the horizon, with a much sharper focus on the bottom line. He thinks "the suits" might improve the finances, but take some of the time-honored passion from the game. A growing number of senior owners are troubled by the assessment and believe it to be a realistic one.

Professional sports teams are significantly different from most other businesses. "In what other business are your competitors your partners?" Reinsdorf asked in the class. A high percentage of a team's revenues comes from the actual games, meaning from the competition within the leagues. For example, the clubs share national television and licensing revenues.

Reinsdorf has a clear, and often stated, goal as the owner of two major sports franchises. He wants to win championships and at least break even. He adds, "I would rather win and break even than to finish second and make $20 million." Realistically, a professional baseball team has to be considered successful if it finishes in the final four and does not lose money. More and more owners subscribe to the Reinsdorf position, believing their ownership is an important contribution to the general welfare of the community.

Always a baseball fan, Reinsdorf bought the White Sox from the legendary Bill Veeck in February 1981 for $19 million. He formed a syndicate of investors and the rest is history. "As business ventures go, owning a baseball team is not a very good one," he cautions, claiming he has about broken even during his long stay on the South Side. Revenues of Major League Baseball have grown dramatically in the past twenty years or so, but so have the operational expenses and especially the player salaries.

Owning an entry in the NBA can be far different, and it can be quite profitable. Reinsdorf bought the Chicago Bulls in 1985, then a troubled franchise, and the club has turned a meaningful profit most of the years since. He was convinced at the time he purchased the Bulls that, with a recently adopted cap on player salaries in the National Basketball Association and some operational changes, the club could become profitable. "I had a long line of friends wanting to invest in the Bulls," he recalls. "I took too many of them in." His ownership of the Bulls experienced an extraordinary run of success with Michael Jordan and friends.

To fully understand Reinsdorf, a shrewd businessman with a law degree from Northwestern University, you first must know that he was born in Brooklyn in 1936, once describing it as "more of a state of mind than a geographical location." As a boy, he did not think he was living in a part of New York City; he lived in Brooklyn, the fourth largest city in the United States. After all, he reasoned, it had its own president, newspaper and, most importantly, its own baseball team, the Brooklyn Dodgers. It also had real diversity—the different races, religions, national origins, and political parties.

During Reinsdorf's formative years, baseball was the only real national sport. Neither the National Basketball Association nor the National Football League had really taken nationwide wings until well after the arrival of Jackie Robinson in 1947. "We lived and died with the Dodgers," he recalled. He credits his parents and his Brooklyn roots for teaching him that discrimination for any reason is just plain wrong and in no one's best interest. He told the students at Princeton that the Brooklyn of his youth had every race and religion, and that he was able to see that all groups had good people and "their share of jerks."

It was Reinsdorf's background that prompted Commissioner Selig and me to ask him to lead Major League Baseball's publicized drive to increase the number of minority employees at every level of the game, both on and off the field. He led the charge with often-stern conviction throughout most of the 1990s, and his efforts resulted in a new awareness and tangible hiring progress. Minorities had a special friend in Jerry Reinsdorf, who freely criticized those owners who he thought had failed to measure up on the minority front. He was never satisfied, even insisting that fines be levied on clubs not meeting agreed- upon hiring targets.

Reinsdorf also pressed the clubs to seek out minority-owned businesses, emphasizing that Major League Baseball wanted them to compete for purchases of goods and services. The results were immediate and encouraging, with the clubs getting a larger pool of suppliers and better quality goods and services at lower prices. Both sides were winning with this newfound relationship, and the game was making new and needed friends among the minority communities. More people of color started to attend baseball games during this period of receptivity. "Both minorities and nonminorities are likely to buy your product if they perceive you to be an equal opportunity company and a contributor to society," Reinsdorf would tell his fellow lords of the realm.

Another leader of the period was John Harrington, the former CEO of the Boston Red Sox, who chaired a majority of the committees of importance to the game. He often told his colleagues at owners' meetings that the people of New England "love the sea, politics, independence, clams, arguing baseball, and not necessarily in that order." He believed a New Englander read the morning newspaper from spring to October, focusing on the Red Sox box score, the weather, and the obituaries.

Harrington was especially sensitive to the image of the game, believing his Red Sox were vital to the city of Boston and to its identity. A poll in 2000 revealed that a compelling 93 percent of the

Boston community agreed with his belief on the importance of the team to the citizens. Only St. Louis has scored as high in polls with its baseball-loving citizenry for the Cardinals.

The Boston Red Sox had fifty-eight consecutive home game sellouts in the 2000 season, and the team has drawn two million spectators for the past fifteen years. That was especially impressive when one remembers that the Red Sox play in the oldest and the smallest park in Major League Baseball, one with fewer than thirty-four thousand seats and relatively few fan comforts.

I believe the Red Sox have an unmatched record of charitable contributions to the Boston area, starting with the ownership of Tom and Jean Yawkey in 1933. They were from the old school of owners, not attempting to maximize profits but rather to keep the game affordable for families. The Yawkeys left their considerable wealth to a Boston Foundation that now gives away millions of dollars to organizations in the Northeast, specializing in education, health care, and youth sports. John Harrington today directs the Yawkey Foundation on a full-time basis.

In Chicago, the White Sox and the Bulls give millions of dollars back to the community for charitable purposes. The Reinsdorf franchises, for example, have refurbished all of the baseball fields and basketball courts in the city parks. The teams also have singled out the Chicago Public Schools to which they have given millions of dollars for teacher -training programs, computers, and the improvement of facilities. Their considerable efforts in philanthropy have drawn praise from the schools and their teachers, and the mayor.

According to Harrington, the Red Sox sell history as well as baseball. He believes the game offers a timeless product, one that is no less exciting today than it was in 1941 when Ted Williams hit .406 and Joe DiMaggio hit safely in fifty-six straight games. He does believe reasonable and periodic change in the game is not only good, but also necessary. He cast the Boston vote for the introduction of new league divisions through realignment, for the addition of a wild card playoff series, and for the introduction of interleague play. He also encouraged the 2001 introduction of an unbalanced schedule, in which each team would play significantly more games against division rivals and fewer games against nondivision rivals. It was designed to heightened rivalries.

More than 83 percent of the fans have said, through national polls, the changes have made the game more interesting and heightened their interest in it. I can say that Harrington, without fail, agonized over any issue of significance, always wanting to be receptive to reasonable change, but mindful of the game's long history and cherished traditions. On many occasions, he forced his fellow owners at American League meetings to debate and resolve the thorny issues that regularly confronted the sport.

The Red Sox philosophy, under the Yawkeys and Harrington, was simple and straightforward, as Harrington would explain: "We do not run the organization to maximize profit; on the contrary, we run the organization to maximize our chances of winning baseball games, while struggling in today's crazy baseball economics to keep baseball affordable family entertainment. We are fiscally prudent, but our goal is only to break even, which is what the financial results show." Boston consistently has one of the largest player payrolls in the American League.

Both Harrington and Reinsdorf have pushed for marketing programs aimed at women and families. "They are the future," Harrington said at one of his last meetings as an owner in 2002. "Baseball must be more affordable than any other sport, and it must be stable and competitive."

Like their counterparts from across the baseball map, Harrington and Reinsdorf have found themselves targeted by the press on occasion. Boston and Chicago have especially aggressive sportsreporters who often give a disproportionate amount of time and space to any hint of controversy. Unfortunately, too many owners and their subordinates fear the media and that can lead management to make unwise decisions. "Members of the media are not accountable for their words," Reinsdorf told the students. "The owners are accountable."

Since most fans either see games in person or on television or hear them on the radio, reporters have to devote their creative energies to what is happening outside the game. They have become like their counterparts on the news side of journalism; they are investigative reporters. I have found most of the reporters who cover Major League Baseball to be uncommonly fair, but a few of them are occasionally difficult. More owners in all professional sports should learn to use a polite "no comment" when in doubt.

The owner of a Major League Baseball club needs to know enough about the game to ask his general manager the right, and often difficult, questions about why certain personnel judgments are necessary; and the owner has the responsibility to be at the table when major financial commitments are made, especially the ones involving large contracts for players. Both Harrington and Reinsdorf agree that the best CEOs in Major League Baseball are the ones who know when and how to delegate to their management teams. An owner who finds he is overriding the general manager on player personnel matters is either off base or in need of a new general manager.

Fortunately, there is a wealth of able and well-educated young men and women who want careers in college and professional sports. And there are growing numbers of gifted older people who are looking for new challenges, second careers. All are anxious to roll up their sleeves and prove themselves. They are male and female, black and white, yellow and brown. They are a diverse group, the kind of individuals who have made the United States a great and progressive nation. Sports administration classes at today's colleges and universities are oversubscribed and have been for quite some time now.

Peter Angelos takes a slightly different view of ownership of a Major League Baseball club. As an attorney who amassed a fortune in the 1980s and 1990s through litigation of worker asbestos damage suits, he remembers the spiritual death suffered by the people of Baltimore when they lost the football Colts to Indianapolis in 1984.

The community openly lobbied for local ownership when the Orioles were put up for sale and sold in 1993. Angelos and his investors thought hometown control would bring the team closer to the public and more clearly demonstrate that a sports franchise is a key community asset. He admits that he never considered the acquisition of the Orioles as an investment, saying there was "always much more to it." He knew the eventual price for the franchise might be much more than economics alone could justify. In the end, Angelos paid a record price of $173 million for the Baltimore club, which raised eyebrows throughout the sporting world.

Angelos did believe, and has insisted, the Orioles had to be run in a businesslike manner. "We all hold our teams in trust for our communities, for our fans and neighbors," he has said. Therefore, he frequently underscores the importance of exposing the game to those of an early age, believing the love of baseball begins at a very young age. He especially delights in the large numbers of youngsters who attend games with their parents at Camden Yards during the summer months.

≈

19

A Time of Change

The face of Major League Baseball has been changed over the past ten years, and some of the naysayers are not especially impressed with the makeover. Fortunately for the thirty clubs, the fans seem to embrace the alterations or at least the great majority do. More than 90 percent of the game's followers like the wild card and the extra tier of playoff games, scientific polls tell us. Those most critical of the changes are fans that admit to being resistant to any form of change and see themselves as being traditionalists, defenders of the game.

Perhaps the most popular move came with the introduction of interleague play in 1997, an idea first advanced by Bill Veeck and Hank Greenberg in 1948. The many competitive possibilities instantly stirred the blood of rabid fans that foresaw the making of a string of heated rivalries. At the urging of the commissioner and the two league presidents, the owners agreed to try three division formats in the American and National Leagues, and the wild card and an extra round of playoff games in 1995. Some owners saw the structural changes as experimental, and not likely to last for more than a couple seasons.

I firmly believed then, and do now, the structural changes came at a time when millions of fans had to be shown that Major League Baseball was not a dinosaur, big and slow and reluctant to change. Commissioner Selig always tells people he listens to the critical voices, but he does like to remind them that baseball, as a social institution, has survived two world wars, a depression, gambling scandals, and numerous collisions involving labor and management. He tends to become a bit defensive when the volume of criticism is too loud on the merits of structural change.

The owners remain convinced the consolidation of umpiring of the American and National Leagues into the Office of the Commissioner in 2000 was a constructive move, arguing that it was the only way to bring about reaffirmation of the rulebook strike zone. I disagreed at the time with the proposed structure, not the objective. I did oppose the merging of administrative responsibilities of the league offices, believing it would lessen the established identities of the leagues, and I conclude it has done that.

Bob Costas says enforcing the strike zone rule gives pitchers a better chance to get ahead of hitters in the count, and that quickens the pace of games. Sandy Alderson, the executive vice president with responsibility for all on-field operations, agrees and reminds the clubs that the game's once-leisurely pace is no longer an asset, but rather a problem. He has growing support from managers, coaches, general managers, and the owners, as the games are growing shorter in length.

Dealing with change is never easy in a game built so much on tradition, and especially when it involves umpires, long known for being cantankerous, free spirits. The 2003 controversy involves "man versus machine," Murray Chass of *The New York Times* has written. For the first time, the men in blue are being graded on their calls of balls and strikes, and the grader is a video camera and computer system. If the system disagrees with 10 percent of an umpire's calls, his performance is considered below standard. Umpires with the highest grades are rewarded with the postseason assignments, which carry added compensation. The umpires, through their union, say the system is flawed, and management disagrees. The disagreement will be adjudicated by an arbitrator, causing continued unrest between the umpires and officials at the commissioner's office in New York.

As a former league president, I salute the efforts of management to bring about greater discipline in the ranks of umpires. Under Richie Phillips, the past umpires union chief, a few of the senior umpires had begun to see themselves as bigger than the players, the game, and certainly the owners. One needs to understand that fans do not pay to see umpires, and the very best ones are largely invisible when at work. They had to be reined in, adhering to many of the same requirements as game officials from the other professional sports. Some baseball umpires in the 1990s even resented having to take annual physical examinations and meeting widely accepted weight standards.

The commissioner insists, and correctly so, the increase in attendance over the past decade is no fluke. He points to the "unprecedented boon" in ballpark construction, and the retro designs that bring back the glorious memories of such remarkable structures as Ebbets Field, the Polo Grounds, and Shibe Park. The days of the cookie cutter design for stadiums are over. It should be noted that the average attendance for a Major League Baseball game in 1959 was 14,105 spectators; today the clubs average 2.5 million fans a season.

With regard to television, the Office of the Commissioner pledges the game will do everything within its power, working with producers, to capture the sights and sounds for the viewing audience, which will provide a more entertaining product. It is obvious that baseball, historically reticent about changing, must be made into a better sport for television. Significantly, even the most popular sports at the college and professional levels have suffered drops in national ratings among the major television networks because of the tremendous growth of cable. Local over-the-air and cable ratings have remained about the same for Major League Baseball in recent years, but the game must increase its viewer base, especially among the young, if it is to maintain its enviable position among the big revenue sports. Advertisers remain fixated on the importance of the youthful consumer and that is not going to change.

Any meaningful discourse on the state of sports and television needs to include clear recognition that the interests of the people have changed, become fragmented, especially in the past twenty years. There are now, for example, burgeoning professional leagues for women in basketball, softball, and soccer, and even golf has its own cable channel. We have witnessed the dramatic emergence of stock car racing and figure skating, both immensely popular with a large number of television viewers. NASCAR, to the surprise of many viewers, is very competitive with professional baseball, basketball, football, and hockey.

The players deserve special recognition for their actions following the national tragedy of September 11, 2001, giving heartfelt expressions of sympathy and support to the fallen firefighters, police, and medical workers, and to their families. The players from the Yankees and the Mets were impacted in a very personal way by the devastation and loss of life at the World Trade Center, but they responded by making immediate visits to the rescue workers at ground zero, bringing prayers and words of comfort.

Difficult as it was, they played the games with the hope they were providing something special, something meaningful, a needed outlet for an anguished city and a sorrowful nation. Somehow the players on the New York teams all looked much older than their years. "I know the games helped in the healing process," Rudolph Giuliani told the players. Certainly, society saw the very real value of athletic competition and the positive influence the people who play the games can provide.

20

Not Your Average Job

In many ways, Brian Cashman is like any chief operating officer of a large business. He makes important personnel decisions, lives within a clearly defined budget, and works for open and productive relationships with the media. He also never forgets the need for profits, which provide opportunities for greater successes.

But Cashman's situation is, at the same time, unique in that he is the general manager of the New York Yankees, arguably the most storied and successful sports franchise on the planet. And he works for George Steinbrenner, one of the most demanding, and often unpredictable, bosses in any business enterprise.

Winning it all, meaning the American League championship and the World Series trophy, is what is expected of the Yankees by their fans and the club owner who resides in Tampa. Anything less is seen as failure within the organization, and failure makes for a long, and painful, off-season, and numerous shuttle flights to Florida and the Yankee offices for strategy meetings with Steinbrenner. The Boss assumes that the rest of the organization (the business operations) will run like a well-oiled machine, with even an occasional miscue frowned upon.

Cashman was named general manager of the Yankees on February 3, 1998, at age 30, a rarity. At the time of his appointment, he had only a decade of experience in the front office of the New York club, but Steinbrenner sensed something special about the one-time intern and his ability to work with people in addressing complex problems. He was an especially good listener and a very quick learner. Members of the hardened press were less sure of the appointment, but willing to give Cashman, known for his humility and openness, a chance.

I very much liked the Steinbrenner appointment of Cashman, who worked quite effectively with the American League staffers, but I did not predict, at the time, that he would last long enough to receive a gold watch from the Yankees. General managers and managers in the Bronx always seemed to be riding a carousel.

But Cashman is an undisputed success story, alternately wearing four World Series championship rings and coming within a single game of having a fifth. During his visit to the class, he opened by reminding the students that winning on the field results in profitability and that enhances your chances for further victories. Winning, he said, expands the fan base, heightens interest and loyalty to the team, and maximizes ticket sales. He also said success at Yankee Stadium leads to greater concession, parking, and memorabilia revenues, all essential to the business plan.

The youthful executive, who could have passed for one of the students at Princeton, further explained that winning championships leads to the generation of more leverage for radio and television fees, sponsorships, and advertising packages. "It is all part of the Yankee equation," he said. "Profitable returns provide the financial latitude to attract, obtain, and equitably compensate quality players and key personnel capable of extending a winning record." In short, winning is an essential ingredient toward becoming and remaining a successful sports franchise, as the Bronx Bombers have proven over the years.

Cashman says the fundamental job of a general manager in Major League Baseball is to build a winning team of associates. The GM needs to have a vision for his team, and be able to effectively communicate that vision to staff members, the people who will be entrusted with its implementation. He clearly must have the total support of the owner. Cashman sees the general manager as an architect, one who is hired to design a winning team in a cost-effective manner.

Once formulated, the general manager then presents his blueprint for action to the team manager, who Cashman regards as the "general contractor," determining what types of players and coaches are needed to achieve the vision, strategy, and goals. His go-to guy is one of the game's finest, Joe Torre. "To ensure success, the general manager must equip the team manager with the appropriate tools to build a winning team for today, and maintain it for tomorrow," he declared at Princeton. Cashman and Torre talk a lot, sometimes appearing to be inseparable.

Specifically, the successful general manager of the 2000s must encircle himself with quality professional people, including seasoned scouts capable of eyeing and rating athletes available within the amateur, international, and professional arenas. He needs a player development director to evaluate, shape, and condition the skills of young players within the structure of six minor league teams, as well as veteran players whose game might need some adjustment.

The Cashmans of the baseball world need a first-class medical team, consisting of doctors, trainers, strength and conditioning coaches, masseurs, a psychologist, and a nutritionist. "Players must have optimal physical and mental strength to be successful," the Yankee GM added.

Cashman admits that not many are able to effectively tolerate the pressure of being a general manager in today's climate, since one is being judged publicly and second-guessed daily. A successful GM realizes early on that he must consult regularly with the owner, explaining any and all matters of importance, and be available to answer the daily and legitimate questions from both the media and the fans.

Cashman likes to quote former Yankee GM and player Gene Michael, who advised him at the time of his appointment to "never lie to the press." It is not only a good policy, I believe, but also the only one in the current climate. "I am a strong advocate of honesty, but it is unnecessary and unwise to respond to every question posed," he said in class. Sometimes a simple "no comment" will suffice, and is the only truthful response to be made at the time. Cashman follows four steps in dealing with the New York media: (1) be honest, (2) be polite, (3) be prepared, and (4) be aware. "As the company's spokesman and representative, deviating from this approach would be committing corporate suicide," he explained. He does not consider his interaction with reporters on a daily basis to be a burden, but rather a unique opportunity to communicate with the team's many customers, the fans.

He regards himself as a businessman, always looking for creative men and women who are well-educated in areas important to the Yankees. He especially likes young people who have traveled the intern route, like he once did, which means they have worked long and hard at the grass roots of an organization. Internships expose youngsters to the realities of professional sports teams, while testing their aptitude for possible careers.

≈

21

The Economic Case of the 2000s

Ron Blum disarmed his student audience at Princeton with his candor and insight, explaining the history of labor relations in Major League Baseball and the impact of the explosion in player salaries in the late 1990s and early 2000s. In subsequent articles for the Associated Press, the veteran sportswriter has pointed to the average annual player salary of more than $2.5 million for MLB, and compared it with the other major professional sports—basketball, hockey, and football. He revealed the player average in the NBA at $4.5 million, the NHL at $1.6 million, and the NFL at $1.2 million.

"When it comes to teams, the Yankees are in a world of their own," Blum wrote, noting their team payroll had been the highest in Major League Baseball for the past four seasons. Owner George Steinbrenner had spent nearly $150 million on players by 2003 opening day. Blum also pointed out that Alex Rodriguez of the Texas Rangers makes more money, $22 million a year, than the entire Tampa Bay team, who earn less than $20 million.

As a sign of the economic times, the number of MLB players making a million dollars or more per year dropped from 413 in

2002 to 385 in 2003. The same trend is likely to be seen in the other professional sports leagues, as the economy continues to take its toll. Most general managers in baseball are assuming they will be asked to do more with less in the immediate future.

I am convinced the recent slowdown in player salaries is attributable to a prolonged slump in the national economy and to the new collective bargaining agreement, not to any form of subtle conspiracy on the part of the owners. Owners of sports teams are not immune from the financial realities of the world, and they have been, with few exceptions, in dire straights in recent years, and many of them are dependent on their businesses and investments away from the games.

The far more interesting question to me is: What will happen after the economic recovery? Will the owners return to their often reckless ways of spending, ignoring the rationale for meaningful restraint? Will they be willing to pay the price, meaning luxury tax penalties, to enhance their chances for victories on the field and possible championships?

There will be growing pressure from impassioned fans to loosen the purse strings, and persuasive pleas from well-read columnists to owners to add an expensive star here and there, which might guarantee pennants for the long-suffering locals. A few owners probably will cave, but certainly not the majority. I am convinced that a growing number of owners believe there is a way to win more games and spend less money on player salaries, subscribing to the highly publicized Billy Beane mode of operation in Oakland. Without question, the A's general manager has caught the attention of owners from the smaller market clubs and elevated their hopes for success on the cheap.

On the other hand, the players are hoping for a strong and speedy economic recovery and a return to the days when owners were willing, even anxious, to pay appreciably more for talent. The great majority of them were supportive of the new labor agreement, mindful of the realities of the day, but they did not surrender their dreams for a return to better times, economically, for players.

22

The Designated Hitter's Time Has Come

In the early 1970s, the owners from the American League were troubled by the dwindling attendance at their ballparks, and by the dreadfully low batting averages being posted by their teams. Spurred by the late Charles O. Finley, then the colorful owner of the Oakland A's, they agreed something had to be done to enliven the game, something dramatic. Thus, the AL owners introduced, after considerable wrangling, the designated hitter in 1973. Its only purpose was to assure a game with more offensive fireworks.

The National League disapproved from the outset and never gave the controversial rule serious consideration, especially since its owners felt their rosters were brimming with excellent hitters and frontline pitchers. Some owners from the senior circuit even thought the purity of the game had been forever tainted.

I always liked and defended the designated hitter, as it gave a few of Major League Baseball's most exciting players extended life at the plate--stars like Al Kaline, George Brett, Harold Baines, Edgar Martinez, Jose Canseco, Chili Davis, Jim Rice, and Paul Molitor. American League fans enthusiastically embraced the innovation, buying increased numbers of tickets and marveling at the newfound offense. The designated hitter had real appeal to many, and it gave the fans from the two leagues even more to argue about. It stirred good-natured competition.

Students of the game recall the 1970s as a time when the game thrived because of players who hit over .350, players who struck forty or more home runs, and players who would steal nearly a hundred bases in a season. Observers say the designated hitter was one of the reasons for the rich spectacle on the field and the enthusiasm in the stands.

Critics of the rule often forget that the designated hitter is used throughout organized baseball, even in Japan, leaving the National League as the single entity not in step with the baseball times, and I know of no serious movement to eliminate the DH elsewhere. As parents will tell you, it gives one more kid a chance to bat, enlivening the game. Going to the plate is a high point for most youngsters and their cheering parents.

But enough is enough. It is time to strike down the designated hitter rule in the American League. It has served its purpose. Without question, the batters of today are bigger and stronger and are pounding home runs at a startling rate. There is no power outage in either the American or National Leagues. Some critics, especially those who like good pitching, complain the explosion of offense in recent years has distorted the game, and they make an arguable case.

The owners in both leagues today hope the designated hitter rule has run its course, and in 1977 they even proposed that it be phased out and replaced with a permanent roster position for each team. The Players Association said no, reasoning that some of the American League's highest paid players would be eliminated. The owners, on the other hand, saw little reason to continue the designated hitter since offensive numbers were sky high.

In all honesty, the owners also saw the potential for salary savings, knowing a DH is usually a veteran, high salaried player, and a new permanent roster player would be young and at the low end of the salary scale. Elimination of the designated hitter might shorten games in the American League a bit, or so officials believe in growing numbers at 245 Park Avenue. Since fans share the officials' desire for shorter games, I am certain there would be little, if any, backlash to the elimination of the designated hitter. I also believe the DH rule will be around for a while longer, since Don Fehr and Gene Orza are certain to balk on the matter.

23

The Reformatted All -Star Game

I was one of the former league presidents the commissioner asked about the idea of giving home-field advantage to the league that won the All -Star Game, and after a couple days of thought, I encouraged him to recommend it to the owners. And he did and they said yes, believing it would give the summer classic a new and needed sense of importance to the fans. The early reaction was overwhelmingly positive from the general public.

It is interesting to note that Commissioner Selig credits William Giles, a longtime president and chairman of the Philadelphia Phillies and the son of a former president of the National League, with the idea for the new format. The owners regarded him as a mainstream colleague, one who had special knowledge, insight, and respect for the game's values and traditions. The vote, by the way, was unanimous, as many of them are when Selig is an active advocate.

As early as 1997, owners in the American League were beginning to express concern about the future of the All-Star Game, long regarded as one of Major League Baseball's two signature events, the other one being the World Series. The television ratings were starting to suffer.

It was not surprising then to learn that Fox Television executives were proactive, offering encouragement to both Commissioner Selig and Don Fehr on the change, believing it would generate appreciably more interest in the game they would televise. All parties from baseball regard Fox as an important partner and an organization that has made a real investment in the future of the sport. The players had early concerns, but finally voted in the affirmative for a two-year experiment starting in Chicago in 2003. The new deal provides for two additional players from each league, bringing the roster total to thirty-two, and gives the players, managers, and coaches a voice in who makes the squads, besides the starters who are selected by the fans.

Selig expects the players to take the All-Star Game far more seriously with so much at stake and, likewise, the managers from the American and National Leagues will feel increased pressure to win for their league advantage. He freely admits that home field advantage in the World Series has been "a significant factor" in the past twenty-five years. The fans certainly can count on seeing the starters, the players they elected, in the All-Star Game for more than a token few innings of play.

The 2002 All-Star Game in Milwaukee ended in an extra inning 7–7 tie, prompting massive criticism from the fans and the media. That had never happened before, and it will never happen again, Commissioner Selig has promised. The managers, Joe Torre of the New York Yankees and Bob Brenly of the Arizona Diamondbacks, ran out of pitchers at Miller Park. Without question, the All-Star Game remains the premier all-star event in professional sports, and it deserves to be saved and improved upon.

Some pundits have attacked the reconfigured format, calling it little more than a public relations gimmick, while others have suggested the integrity of the World Series has been served up for the benefit of higher summer television ratings. Both arguments are overblown. Quite frankly, Bud Selig had to do something to give the game more meaning, and the new format might do just that. Certainly, it deserves a try since it is not cast in stone. There was a time when the American and National Leagues played the All-Star Game for pride, rings, and bragging rights alone, with the presidents even giving pep talks to the teams before the game. That clearly is no longer the case.

Several members of the 2003 All-Star Game squads suggested giving each winning player fifteen thousand dollars, with the money going to a charity. They were uneasy about continuing the home field advantage for the World Series, and especially liked the idea of linking the summer classic incentive with charity. The All-Star Game festivities already generate a considerable sum for charitable purposes. Owner Jerry Reinsdorf said the White Sox gave the nearly one million dollars they received from the All-Star Day workout in Chicago to youth baseball, and a like amount was donated to Major League Baseball Charities.

≈

24

The Rose Dilemma

Younger baseball fans know more about the exploits of Pete Rose as a gambler than as a player. The man with the most base hits in Major League Baseball history, even more than Ty Cobb, is usually recognized in the media as the tarnished star of the once-dominant Cincinnati Reds, who reportedly bet on baseball games as a manager and was banned from the game fourteen years ago by the late Bart Giamatti, a commissioner known for fairness.

Bud Selig has a real dilemma on his hands, and has had for quite some time, knowing that every fan poll taken in the past decade has favored some kind of return for Rose; and yet as the commissioner of America's pastime he has an obligation to do what is right, regardless of political consequences. There is no shortage of emotionally held views on the issue of Pete Rose, even with the passage of time. Academics are divided on what they regard as fair in the Rose case.

Realizing that no decision will totally satisfy the multitude of those with strongly held opinions, I believe the time has come to reinstate Rose, making him eligible for election to the Hall of Fame by the baseball writers, who cast the ballots. The writers will approve Rose on a closer vote than many think. I do not believe, however, that he should be allowed to return as a manager or coach of a Major League Baseball club.

Americans are forgiving people, and they clearly believe in giving second chances to sports figures. Rose, I contend, has served his time, even though his explanation of what he did, or did not do, and when, is less than compelling. His explanation has been fuzzy, as even some of his player friends have admitted. He has admitted, for example, to having a gambling problem and then saying the evidence against him was incomplete and his accusers were biased.

But no one can dispute the fact that Rose had 4,256 hits, far more than the 3,000 hits thought to guarantee election to the Hall of Fame. I must admit to being influenced by Cal Ripken, who feels that Rose should be allowed in the Hall of Fame. One of the few who has scaled the 3,000-hit barrier, Ripken is a person of unquestioned integrity and one who enjoys universal respect among present and former players. I always held him in the highest regard during my six-year tour as league president. Ripken is uncertain whether Rose should be allowed back in the game. Interestingly, Ripken is one of the seven players with more than three thousand hits and four hundred home runs, and he played the infield for the Baltimore Orioles for twenty-one seasons, retiring after the 2001 season.

One of the reasons Selig has been slow to come down on the Rose matter is his steadfast respect for Giamatti and the time he spent as commissioner agonizing over what he thought was just and in the game's best interest. Former Commissioner Fay Vincent, once a deputy to Giamatti, objects to a possible return for Rose. In any event, some critics believe the decision on Rose should have been made years ago. I disagree.

I further believe the time is right to revisit the case of Shoeless Joe Jackson of the infamous Chicago Black Sox. The late Ted Williams went to his final resting place believing that baseball had a moral obligation to reconsider the facts involved in the case, which, at the time, made a clear distinction between gambling and other misdeeds in society. Gambling brought into question the fundamental integrity of the game, or so concluded Kenesaw Mountain Landis after the 1919 scandal. Judge Landis barred Jackson and seven of his teammates from baseball for life. "Baseball is something more than a game to an American boy," he said at the time. "It is his training field for life work."

Williams insisted on meeting with Commissioner Selig, Len Coleman, and me to make a heartfelt case for Jackson during one of his last visits to Cooperstown. I met with him as president of the American League, and he told me other senior members of the Hall of Fame shared his sentiments.

25

A Thought on Sammy Sosa

Sammy Sosa seemed to live a charmed life, as fans, home and away, cheered his enormous feats. During his riveting home run chase with Mark McGwire in 1998, he, in the final analysis, won the popularity contest while finishing a close second in round trippers to the massive St. Louis first baseman.

The only player to hit 60 or more home runs in three seasons, Sosa especially thrilled and entertained fans with his towering rockets off the bat, with his spirited sprints to his right field playing position, and even with his good natured hawking of Pepsi products on national television commercials. He was a modern day natural, one of the two or three most recognizable and marketable faces in the game.

Then came June 3, 2003 when the bat he was using at Wrigley Field against the Tampa Bay Devil Rays exploded and the umpires found cork. The trademark Sosa smile was gone as he said it was a mistake, that he had used the corked bat during batting practice and picked it up by accident and used it during the game. He offered an immediate apology to the fans.

The media went ballistic, from coast to coast, with more than a few of the writers tagging Sosa as a cheat, who had forfeited his chance to be considered for the Hall of Fame. ESPN saturated the airways with Sosa reactions, rumors, and purported insights for two days and nights, non-stop. After the hearing on the Sosa appeal of eight games, Major League Baseball President Bob DuPuy said he was convinced the incident was a mistake and was impressed with Sosa's remorse, but he said a player must be accountable for his own equipment meeting the well established rules. His suspension was reduced by a game by DuPuy and the punishment was consis-tent with similar player transgressions over the past twenty years.

The night Sosa was ejected for use of a corked bat, 76 of his other bats were taken and X-rayed by Major League Baseball, and nothing illegal was found in any of them. The Hall of Fame in-spected five Sosa bats at Cooperstown and each was declared clean.

Without a doubt, the media overreacted, but that was both pre-dictable and understandable. Sammy Sosa is big, no huge, about as important as one gets in the world of professional athletics. Fur-thermore, he is a first ballot Hall of Famer, a fellow who has swatted more than 500 home runs. A couple of former players got time on radio and television and said a great hitter, like Sosa, would never mistake a corked bat from an uncorked one. The Yankees, who came to Chicago for an interleague series of games on the North Side after the incident, without exception, gave the Cubs slugger the benefit of the doubt. Manager Joe Torre even took time to extol Sosa's contributions to the game of baseball.

I remain convinced that Sammy Sosa is what he appears to be, a genuinely nice person, who made a bad mistake. But I predict it will be the last such mistake; Sosa and the game he represents have too much to lose for any reoccurrence. His legacy has not been permanently scarred; it has been temporarily blemished, and there will be those who forever will remember and remind us of his un-fortunate lapse.

26

The Challenge Facing College Athletics

Like any former university president, I cannot resist the opportunity to give a few observations on the state of college athletics, since it has clear implications for society and professional sports. First, I must admit that I did my share to contribute to the enormity of the problem by bringing big-time football and basketball coaches to West Virginia University and the University of Kansas.

Among my hires were Don Nehlen and Gale Catlett at WVU, and Larry Brown and Roy Williams at KU. I even built a massive football stadium during my days at Morgantown. For the record, Nehlen and Catlett each coached Mountaineer football and basketball, respectively, for more than twenty years and for a record number of school victories; and Brown coached the Jayhawks to an NCAA national basketball championship in 1988 and, as his successor, Williams was one of the three most successful college coaches in terms of wins in the country.

It is tough to know where to start, but I must point to the economic difficulties facing institutions of higher learning in 2003. The picture is so bleak that experienced headhunters report a sharp drop in interest among likely candidates for college and university presidencies, and a survey taken in 2002 found nearly half of the CEO participants were considering early retirement or doing something else not related to higher education.

Few major colleges and universities in the United States have escaped crippling budget cuts, soaring enrollments, and hefty tuition and fee increases during the 2002–2003 school year. Without question, states, large and small, are drowning in a sea of red ink, are having real problems paying bills, and are in the worst shape in more than twenty-five years. And even with some economic recovery, next year appears to be at least as tough as 2003, when 47 of the 50 states had revenues that were short of original estimates, some by as much as 38 percent.

At least forty states reduced projected budgets by more than $17 billion, and higher education and social welfare programs were among the hardest hit in 2003. Simply stated, the basic costs of inflation and population growth are not being funded, and academic quality is being wiped out at many state institutions of higher learning. The likelihood of increased state taxes appears to be remote at this point in time, with most politicians refusing to even consider the possibility. With average double-digit increases for tuition and fees for a third consecutive year, a growing number of students are being priced out of the market. More and more parents are surrendering their dreams of seeing their sons and daughters graduate from college and having the opportunities they never enjoyed.

Furthermore, state schools are receiving a smaller and smaller proportion of tax dollars. Since 1980, the share of state revenue used for higher education has dipped from 44 percent to below 30 percent. Lawmakers, in large numbers, believe higher education is a private good that should be supported more by students and private donors than by state appropriations. I believe America is risking its clear educational advantage, which leaders over the years have regarded as central to global competitiveness. I further believe college affordability is a real issue, and it will remain so for the foreseeable future. A free society, like ours, cannot afford to lose able and inquiring minds.

Given the bleak economic realities of the day, it is easy to understand why a growing number of faculty members from across the country are enraged over the amount of money being spent on college athletics. They regard the system as out of control and threatening academic integrity. Specifically, faculty senates are condemning the arms race of expenditures for coaches' salaries and new stadiums and arenas.

College presidents agree with their faculties and with their calls for reform. But few presidents and athletic directors expect any real change in the near future, realizing that athletic competition is as popular as ever with the alumni, students, the general public, and the politicians who have reduced academic budgets. Some school boosters even equate institutional quality with athletic team wins and losses.

It is increasingly difficult to explain to the public, let alone members of the academic community, why a college football or basketball coach should make a million dollars a year while the rest of the institution is financially starved. Zero salary increases for faculty and staff, for example, were common at many colleges and universities in 2002–2003. Approximately twenty college football coaches, and about the same number of basketball coaches, earn a million dollars a year or more, making them the highest paid public employees. (Presidents usually make a third of that, or less.)

A surprisingly large number of colleges and universities have started stadium and arena construction or renovation projects, totaling more than $4.8 billion, while maintenance for academic buildings is virtually nonexistent at many campuses. Faculty members resent the apparent disproportionate influence of alumni and television on college athletic programs.

It is increasingly difficult to remain silent when certain college presidents talk about "the bright side of intercollegiate athletics," referring with almost reverence to the many lifelong values learned by the student-athletes from these programs. And what are we, and the student athletes, reading and hearing about?

Item: The Atlantic Coast Conference agreed in May 2003 to expand from nine to twelve schools, positioning itself to become one of the largest moneymakers in the NCAA. According to news accounts, the expanded conference would likely produce more than $120 million in annual revenue and guarantee its long-term future. The expanded alignment would permit two divisions and a football championship game for national television, which might generate an additional seven to twelve million dollars. It also could add another round of play to the already popular ACC basketball tournament, increasing its revenue by more than two million dollars. The motive for the reconfiguration clearly was financial, not academic.

The ACC wanted Miami, Syracuse, and Boston College to leave the Big East Conference for the new arrangement. The appeal of the three institutions is understandable. Boston has the sixth largest television market; and Miami stands at number seventeen, and it has a powerhouse football program. Syracuse offers luster as the men's 2003 national basketball champion.

The Big 12 Conference, formerly the Big 8, changed its membership eight years ago when it took in Texas, Texas A&M, Texas Tech, and Baylor, resulting in the demise of the old Southwest Conference. The Big 12, by the way, hopes to grow its annual revenues to more than $100 million within a couple years. In the spirit of full disclosure, I need to report that I favored the enlargement of the old Big 8 Conference as chancellor of the University of Kansas, rationalizing it was the only way KU could remain athletically competitive and have the revenue to pay its bills. I also thought the four Texas universities were compatible with the academic standards, values, and objectives of the Big 8 schools. Significantly, the

Southwest Conference was in disarray long before any discussions with the Big 8.

People are surprised to learn that big-time athletic programs do not guarantee bottom-line success. Of the 117 schools playing in the NCAA's top-level Division 1-A, over half run deficits and only twenty-five to thirty institutions actually turn a profit.

When Cedric Dempsey, the past president of the NCAA, visited with my students he expressed concern about the amount of resources being spent for athletic programs. "We have more dollars in our budgets than ever before," he said. "So much so that the general public, the media, and many in our institutions see an enormous gap between the principle of amateurism we profess and the growing commercialism we practice." He said the so-called arms race for facilities, coaches' salaries, and program enhancements is putting many colleges and universities in debt, and perhaps putting the educational infrastructures at risk. "All this, while student-athletes play without pay and wonder when they will share in this new wealth," he added. Like the growing legions of faculty, Dempsey worries about the increasing and obvious disconnect between college sports and the college mission.

Clearly, millions of Americans like the perceived qualities of college sports. They admit to being taken by the special relationship between athletic participation and academic pursuit that the vast majority of student-athletes demonstrate. Dempsey, once an athletic director at the University of Arizona, insists that college sports should never become professional sports. "Maintaining that 'clear line of demarcation between college and professional sports' is a mandate that remains as relevant today as it did when those words were made part of the association's basic purpose more than 90 years ago," he told the class.

Members of the United States Senate from six states wrote to the CEOs of Miami, Syracuse, and Boston College, saying their departure from the Big East Conference would undermine the integrity of intercollegiate athletics, be harmful to Title IX women's athletic programs, and send a troubling message to student-athletes across America. The senators specifically asked the university presidents to consider the message their decisions to leave would send to student-athletes about the values of intercollegiate athletics. "What message do we send to student-athletes when decades of history can be destroyed as a sole result of economic considerations? The wrong one," they wrote.

The senators took especially sharp aim at the CEOs of the Atlantic Coast Conference, saying they had deserted the qualities that made intercollegiate athletics great, and that is the greatest shame of the entire affair. I believe the move to enlarge the ACC at the expense of the Big East will now reignite the always unpleasant debate on pay for student-athletes.

When it was all said and done, the ACC voted in June 2003 to take Miami and Virginia Tech, the Big East's two dominant football schools. Boston College and Syracuse were left in the dust, even after the ACC had completed required site visits to the campuses weeks earlier. Virginia Tech was a late entry, becoming part of a compromise suggested by the University of Virginia president who was under enormous political pressure in his state. The seven-week courtship between the ACC and Miami ended in late June 2003 when the Florida school announced its intention to leave the Big East and join Virginia Tech in the reconfigured conference.

Unfortunately, the ACC has sent an undeniable message, one that was heard across the nation. In truth, dollars, not academic values, collegiality, or even substantive commonality, decide conference alignments. One can readily understand why faculty members are unusually restive on the matter of athletic program priorities, and why students are growing more and more cynical about the system. The proposed expansion was first announced, for example, when the students were not even on campus, let alone consulted. Without question, some considerable damage has been done in several important campus quarters.

In recent years, I have asked college and university presidents about the direction they believe intercollegiate athletics should be traveling. All are admittedly troubled and, at the same time, realistic, seeing the enormity of support for big and winning programs with alumni, students, and the general public, and the political structure. They do sense a real growing unease among faculty and student groups, and they expect representatives from these groups to become far more active and vocal in the future, especially with the reduced institutional resources for academic programs.

More than a few of the CEOs wish they could roll back the clock and reshape their programs in college athletics. They talk about a return to certain core values, a simpler time, a greater appreciation for the athlete as a student. More than a few of them have pointed longingly to the Ivy League where there is a model that has passed the test of time, one that embodies many of the values they regard as both admirable and needed in intercollegiate athletics. But given their heavy institutional investments in facilities, coaches' salaries, and the resulting indebtedness, the presidents of Division I-A schools are not likely to move, in any serious way, toward an Ivy League-like structure. They will encourage certain substantive academic reforms, but almost all of the presidents feel their options for sweeping change are few and limited.

The Ivy League is unique, as Princeton University athletic director Gary Walters likes to explain:

> There are no athletic scholarships; all financial aid is based on need. The student-athletes are competing for the love of the game and for their institutions, not because they are forced to fulfill certain obligations of an athletic scholarship contract.

The student-athletes go through the same admission process as all other students, which means they are representative of the student body.

Athletic activity is tightly regulated, limiting the student-athletes to only twelve days of practice in the nontraditional season, compared to forty-eight days for other Division I programs.

Generally, Ivy League athletic contests are scheduled for the weekends, thus reducing conflicts with classroom and other educational activities.

≈

27

Sports and Modern Journalism

America's most widely read newspaper would not be in existence without a heavy emphasis on sports reporting, or so said the founder of *USA TODAY* during his visit with my students at Princeton University. Allen H. Neuharth minced no words: to be successful, the new national publication had to offer a comprehensive sports section, one that focused sharply and effectively on the interests of the millions of readers who first turn to the sports section. Also central components to the Gannett Company gamble would be colorful and tightly edited sections dealing with national and international news and editorial views, business, and entertainment.

Neuharth, the former chairman of Gannett, once started a statewide sports paper in 1954 in his native South Dakota. Twenty-two months after printing its first edition, *SoDak Sports* was out of business. "Our circulation was a success," he told the class. "But our advertising bombed." He remained convinced, however, of the importance of sports to the general public and to newspaper readers.

On September 15, 1982, Al Neuharth launched *USA TODAY,* which was to become a national newspaper that would attract millions of readers, including "many of the television generation who were then nonreaders." Neuharth and cable visionary Ted Turner have had, I believe, a greater impact on American journalism than any other two people in the past 50 years. And sports have played an important role in their awe-inspiring success.

Furthermore, those men and women who today direct the nation's media outlets are convinced that the impact of college and professional sports will continue to grow; there is no serious thought of lessening the amount of time and space devoted to sporting events. It is a matter of fundamental economics.

≈

28

The Importance of Competitiveness

In 2002, *The Sporting News* named Rod Thorn the NBA's Executive of the Year, leading Commissioner Stern to call him someone who thoroughly understands "all aspects of college and professional sports." When the president and general manager of the New Jersey Nets speaks, he commands an attentive audience. Students at Princeton gave him high marks for both substance and presentation.

There is no substitute for a competitive product, regardless of the sport, he told the class. The Nets have made it to the NBA championship series in both 2002 and 2003, which explains the unparalleled enthusiam for basketball in the state of New Jersey.

Being competitive in modern professional sports means a club must be able to attract and retain frontline talent, and that is, more often than not, quite expensive. The Nets clearly made the point in 2003, giving guard Jason Kidd a 6-year, $103 million contract to remain in East Rutherford. The NBA all-star is central to future championship runs by the New Jersey Nets. Thorn also added center Alonzo Mourning to the team as a free agent, and that was not inexpensive. Importantly, the fans of the Nets are energized and believe in management's commitment to win.

Still, Thorn worries about the future of the franchise without a new, fan friendly area. A professional basketball team no longer can compete for long without a modern facility, he believes, especially given the growing competitiveness of the sports business. The Nets are pressing for a new downtown arena in Newark, but progress has been slow because of the struggling economy. Most polls show unquestioned support for the proposal and the Nets.

An All-American basketball player at West Virginia University in 1962, Thorn also worries that professional basketball, football, hockey, and baseball are more and more corporate sports, ones that have priced out untold millions of fans. "Professional basketball must keep the game before the people, and live, in-person audiences are very important," he said during his campus visit. He did point to the importance of the WNBA in providing excellent basketball at family prices. Thorn is a unique sports figure, having experience as an NBA player, coach, general manager, league vice president, and club CEO.

≈

29

Added Thoughts

One has to wonder what is going on at the big basketball schools when a small Baptist institution had a head coach who allegedly tried to persuade his assistants and players to lie about NCAA infractions and the tragic death of a player.

The ghoulish episode involving the remains of baseball great Ted Williams serves to remind us all of the importance of treating the legacy and memories of our deceased elders with vigilant sensitivity and deserved respect.

What many fans opposed—or even feared—the introduction of divisional play and the wild card, brought baseball to its most compelling regular season in modern memory in 2003. With more than half of the thirty teams battling for post-season berths to the very end, attendance soared back to the 2002 level, even after wet weather and the struggling economy had hurt attendance during the first half of the season.

The pace of the game quickened in 2003, too, with an average nine-inning contest lasting two hours, forty-six minutes. That came within a minute of commissioner Selig's stated objective, and he credited the players, managers, and umpires.

Another dose of positive news in 2003 was word that regular-season television viewership was up, according to both Fox network and the always-important Nielsen ratings. Without question, national marketers understood what was at play as baseball laid plans for its biggest event, the World Series. The Series commanded, on average, 325,000 dollars per thirty-second advertising spot in the first five games, an increase of eight percent over 2002. The 2003 season was magical for fans and marketers alike.

≈

In October 2003, the Atlantic Coast Conference struck again, this time taking Boston College as a twelfth member. The reason was obvious: The ACC needed another school to meet an NCAA requirement that only conferences with at least twelve teams may schedule a lucrative conference championship game. Miami and Virginia Tech had been added to the conference's previous nine teams in June, and will begin ACC competition in 2004.

Readings

Baseball Encyclopedia. Eighth edition. New York: Macmillan, 1990.

Budig, Gene A. *A Game of Uncommon Skill.* Westport, CT: Oryx Press, 2002.

Costas, Bob. *Fair Ball.* New York: Broadway Books, 2000.

Danielson, Michael N. *Home Team: Professional Sports and the American Metropolis.* Princeton, NJ: Princeton University Press, 1997.

Drury, James. *The Leadership Vacuum in Professional Sports.* Chicago: Spencer Stuart, 2000.

Fort, Rodney. *Sports Economics,* New York: Prentice Hall, 2002.

Gorman, Jerry, and Kirk Calhoun. *The Name of the Game, The Business of Sports.* New York: John Wiley & Sons, Inc., 1994.

Halberstam, David. *The Breaks of the Game.* New York: Alfred A. Knopf, 1981.

Helyar, John. *Lords of the Realm.* New York: Random House, 1994.

Kahn, Roger. *October Men.* New York: Harcourt, 2003.

Kern, William, Editor. *The Economics of Sports.* Kalamazoo, MI: W.E. Upjohn Institute for Employment Research, 2000.

Knight Foundation. *A New Beginning for a New Century.* Report of the Knight Foundation Commission on Intercollegiate Athletics, Charlotte, NC, March 1993.

Kuhn, Bowie. *Hardball.* New York: Times Books, 1987.

Levin, Richard and others. *The Report of the Independent Members of the Commissioner's Blue Ribbon Panel on Baseball Economics,* July 2000.

Lomax, Michael E. *Black Baseball Entrepreneurs, 1860–1901.* Syracuse, NY: Syracuse University Press, 2003.

MacPhail, Lee. *My 9 Innings.* Westport, CT: Meckler Books, 1989.

Masteralexis, Lisa. *Principles and Practice of Sport Management.* Gaithersburg, MD: Aspen Publishers, 1998.

Miller, Marvin. *A Whole Different Ballgame: The Inside Story of Baseball's New Deal.* New York: Simon and Schuster, 1991.

Noll, Roger, and Andrew Zimbalist. *Sports, Jobs and Taxes: The Economic Impact of Sports Teams and Stadiums.* Washington, DC: Brookings Institution Press, 1997.

Quirk, James, and Rodney Fort. *Hard Ball: The Abuse of Power in Pro Team Sports.* Princeton, NJ: Princeton University Press, 1999.

Quirk, James, and Rodney Fort. *Pay Dirt: The Business of Professional Team Sports.* Princeton, NJ: Princeton University Press, 1992.

Rampersad, Arnold. *Jackie Robinson, A Biography.* New York: Alfred A. Knopf, 1997.

Ritter, Lawrence S. *Lost Ballparks*. New York: Viking Penguin, 1992.

Scully, Gerald. *The Business of Major League Baseball*. Chicago: University of Chicago Press, 1989.

Seymour, Harold. *Baseball: The Golden Age*. New York: Oxford University Press, 1971.

Staudohar, Paul. *The Sports Industry and Collective Bargaining*. Ithaca, NY: ILR Press, 1989.

Staudohar, Paul. *Playing for Dollars: Labor Relations and the Sports Business*. Ithaca, NY: ILR Press, 1996.

Swirsky, Seth. *Baseball Letters*. New York: Kodansha International, 1996.

Tygiel, Jules. *Baseball's Greatest Experiment*. New York: Oxford University Press, 1983.

Veeck, Bill. *Veeck as in Wreck*. New York: G.P. Putnam's Sons, 1962.

Vincent, Fay. *The Last Commissioner*. New York: Simon and Schuster, 2002.

Whitford, David. *Playing Hardball*. New York: Doubleday, 1993.

Zimbalist, Andrew. *Baseball and Billions: A Probing Look Inside the Business of Our National Pastime*. New York: Basic Books, 1994.

Zimbalist, Andrew. *Unpaid Professionals*. Princeton, NJ: Princeton University Press, 1999.

Zimbalist, Andrew. *May the Best Team Win: Baseball Economics and Public Policy*. Washington, DC: Brookings Institution Press, 2003.

About the Author

GENE A. BUDIG was appointed the seventh president of Major League Baseball's American League in 1994, and oversaw the operations of 14 clubs for six years and the construction of $2.1 billion worth of new ballparks. Prior to baseball, he headed three major state universities, Illinois State University, West Virginia University, and the University of Kansas, and over a 23-year period was responsible for the educational programs of 520,000 students. A graduate of the University of Nebraska, where he was a full professor at age 32, he joined the faculty at Princeton University and taught from 2000 to 2002, when he left to become a Scholar in Residence at The College Board in New York. He is a retired Major General in the Air National Guard/United States Air Force.

137